The Conquest of Kanchi

(Kanchi Kaveri)

The Conquest of Kanchi
(Kanchi Kaveri)

RAMASHANKAR RAY

Translated by
Debi Prasad Padhi
Gurudev Meher

BLACK EAGLE BOOKS
Dublin, USA | Bhubaneswar, India

Black Eagle Books
USA address:
7464 Wisdom Lane
Dublin, OH 43016

India address:
E/312, Trident Galaxy, Kalinga Nagar,
Bhubaneswar-751003, Odisha, India

E-mail: info@blackeaglebooks.org
Website: www.blackeaglebooks.org

First International Edition Published by
Black Eagle Books, 2024

THE CONQUEST OF KANCHI
(Kanchi Kaveri)
by **RAMASHANKAR RAY**
Translated by **Debi Prasad Padhi** & **Gurudev Meher**

Translation Copyright © Debi Prasad Padhi & Gurudev Meher

All rights reserved. No part of this publication may be reproduced, stored in a retrieval system, or transmitted, in any form or by any means, electronic, mechanical, photocopying, recording or otherwise without the prior permission of the publisher.

Cover & Interior Design: Ezy's Publication

ISBN- 978-1-64560-549-2 (Paperback)
Library of Congress Control Number: 2024937504

Printed in the United States of America

DRAMATIS PERSONAE

MALE

Purushottam Dev	King of Odisha
Bidyanidhi	Minister
Natabara Acharya	Jester
Godabari Mishra	Royal Preceptor
Rudreswar	Royal Astrologer
Ballabha	Chief Courtier
Birabala	Commander in Chief
Meghabarna	Guard
Dasarathi Das	Chief Cook of Lord Jagannath

Sutradhara, Nata, Five Bramhins, milkmen, Guard, soldiers, Musician and his troupe, courtiers

Kalabareswar	King of Kanchi
Dhiraprajnya	Minister of Kanchi
Bajrananda	Commander in Chief of Kanchi

Courtiers, Guard

FEMALE

Bidyullata	Queen of Kanchi
Padmavati	Princess of Kanchi
Sasikala, Suryabala	Maids and attendants of the Princess
Bhadra	Nun
Saramali	Attendant and gardener
Maniki	A Milkmaid of Odisha

Nati, Milkmaid,
A village women

Foreword

This book is a translation of the play *Kanchi Kaveri* or *Padmavati* by Ram Shankar Ray (1857-1931), the first successful Odia playwright. *Kanchi Kaveri* was written in 1880 and first performed on February 7, 1881.

Translation is concerned with rendering a text in one language into another language. The need for translation is two-fold: the reader's necessity, and the writer's desire. When a person wishes to know something written in a language which he/she does not understand, it is the need of a reader. Alternatively, a writer might like to communicate something to persons who do not know his/her language. This is the need of the writer. In either case, lack of knowledge is a barrier to communication. Translation serves as a bridge in overcoming this barrier. It is generally believed that an ideal translation must reproduce the full sense of the original text, omitting nothing, and adding nothing. It is also expected that a translation should not ignore the style of the original. To be able to communicate the meaning of the original text in a style similar to the original text makes translation quite a challenging task. It is also believed that a good translation should not read like a translation at all, but seem like an original text. That is why, a translator must have an excellent knowledge of the language from which the translation is being made. He/she must fully understand its nuances and finer aspects.

Translation of a dramatic text has unique dimensions. Drama is a complex form of art. It is both a literary art and a performing art. It is a written text known as 'script' to be read and enjoyed like poetry or a novel and at the same time to be performed in the theatre for an audience to watch and enjoy. It is multi-dimensional because it incorporates other literary genres such as poetry and music besides prose. In poetry and fiction, the writer may take liberties with time and space. But a playwright cannot violate the basic principles of stagecraft the unity of time, place and action lest he should lose hold of the attention of the spectators. The playwright has to take care of dialogues appropriate to characters, time and place. Dialogue is delivered in a particular time and place and highlights the situation or modifies it. It also reveals the dynamics of the relationships among characters while the dialogue derives its full significance within the total context of the play. Therefore, in Aristotle's definition of Tragedy, diction is an important element. Moreover, tone of voice, facial expressions, costumes, background scenery and inclusion of songs lend lasting appeal to the performance of a play. Thus, a play is not just a linguistic form but also an extra-linguistic situation. All these factors make rendering a dramatic text in the Source Language into a Target Language challenging. The complexity of the problem of translation can be assessed from the fact that the same play with the same actors and the same director can be applauded on one day and criticized the next.

    The quality of a piece of translated work is always under the scanner. The translation was simply seen as the rendering of the source language (SL) texts into an equivalent target language (TL) product. The success of the translated piece was measured in terms of whether it was a faithful or beautiful translation. In her introduction to the

2001 special issue of the journal Metamorphosis dedicated to drama translation, Kiki Gounaridou discusses the potential relationship of faithfulness or unfaithfulness to the original text and wonders about the nature of a drama translation: "Is there such a thing as 'literal' translation'? What is the difference between translation and adaptation?" She also raises a question that is often the centre of theatre translation studies today: "Can theatricality and meaning be carried and transmitted through translation from one dramatic text to the other, from one culture to another? And is translation a copy or is it an interpretation?" She writes: "In many ways, translation falls within the larger framework of interpretation and mimesis: like theatre, translation itself is double talk, both present and not present, both reality and fiction." According to Luigi Pirandello, a modern Italian playwright, faithfulness is an impossible concept since translators "falsify" the original text. But the Russian writer Gogol sees an ideal translation as a "completely transparent glass through which one can see the original". Thus, he supports faithfulness as the all-dominant criterion.

The process of translation is very intricate. How far the textual material in the SL has been replaced by TL equivalents depends on the process through which the translator produces his work. A translator has to perform three distinct roles during the act of translation: (a) the role of a reader trying to grasp the import of the SL text, (b) the role of a bilingual translator trying to find the exact expressions in the TL and (c) the role of a writer of the translated text. The translator first decodes the original text in order to grasp and interpret the message as a reader, and transforms this message into its structurally clear forms of text in the TL as an effective writer.

A translator encounters several curious problems while translating a play. The translator usually creates a text for a group of readers whose language and culture differ from those of the writer and readers of the SL text. This difference in language and culture creates serious problems for a translator because, on the one hand, he/she has to take into account the form and the content of the SL text and on the other, the entire system of communicative features associated with the language of the translated (TL) text. The principle of equivalence is primarily based on the basic assumption that identical structures cannot exist between two languages. There are no exact correspondences between related linguistic items across languages. It is rather impossible to find a one-to-one correspondence between the vocabulary, grammar, style etc. of two languages. Yet each language has the potential to communicate the message that has been expressed in some other language. It is this potential of expressing the same message across languages having different vocabulary and grammar that is exploited by a translator.

A translator has to be equipped with the necessary skills required for his work. If the plays are translated without keeping 'performance' in mind, the main focus on linguistic fidelity or faithfulness to the language of the original will suffer. If the translation is too literal it sounds 'bookish' and unperformable. The primary requirement of any translator is proficiency in both the SL and TL. S/he should also be well-informed about the relationship between drama and theatre. It should be kept in mind that S/he is not merely translating a play from one language to another but also transforming the cultural and historical context as well as the dramatic conventions from the SL into the TL. To overcome the difficulties in translation, the translator has to keep certain things in mind: (i) the potential audience, (ii) cultural symbols, (iii) names of characters and places, (iv) historical context, (v) the use of appropriate language and (vi) performability. The production of a play for a rural audience or an elite audience needs different theatrical conventions to meet the expectations of the audience. If they recognize something familiar like names of characters and places their enjoyment increases. Hence historical and cultural contexts have to be taken care of.

A play is seen as well as heard. As a play is seen the translator has to keep in mind its visual elements: setting, costumes, the movements of actors, their gestures and expressions. As a play is also heard the dialogue must have the necessary rhythm, intonation, voice modulations, speed of delivery and pauses. How these elements are to be incorporated in the TL will depend a lot on the sensitivity and creativity of the translator.

Drama and theatre have their origins in the cultural settings of the past and the vicissitudes of the present. The theatre tradition has been part of the ritual and social life of the people embracing the totality of their way of life, habits, attitudes and propensities. Like the novel and the short story, the modern drama was the product of Odia authors' exposure to English literature. Art is more than just self-expression and self-communication. It allows the individual to escape into the refuge of fantasy and leave behind the stress and strain of life. Drama as well as theatre has a great influence on society.

Ramashankar Ray (1858-1917) is credited as the first successful playwright. He happened to witness a Bengali play *Ramabhishek* (*Coronation of Rama*) being staged in Cuttack in 1878 and resolved to write a drama in Oriya. His first play, *Kanchi-Kaveri* was first staged on February

7, 1881. *Kanchi Kaveri* has been acknowledged as the first full-fledged Odia play and Ramashankar as the first Odia playwright. He chose as his hero Gajapati Purushottam Dev, the illustrious king of the Surya dynasty of Odisha. Through his historic war with the king of Kanchi, Saluva Narasimha Dev, Ray has depicted the Odia's patriotism. The play won the hearts of audiences instantly by its popular nationalistic theme and attractive presentation.

Though it is not a completely historical play, it is beyond doubt that it depicts the glorious history of Odisha. The legend of King Purushottam Dev's love for Padmavati, the princess of Kanchi, the invasion of Kanchi and the eventual wedding of Purushottam Dev and Padmavati is running the round in Odisha. There is a brief record of the wedding of Purushottam Dev and Padmavati in the *Madala Panji*, the official chronicle of the Jagannath Temple, Puri. In the eighteenth century, poet Purushottam Das had written a long narrative poem on the love story of Purushottam Dev and Padmabati. Rangalal Banerjee, a Bengali poet had written a long narrative poem named *Kanchi Kaveri* depicting the same love story. Ramashankar might have gone through all these texts and been inspired by the dramatic themes of romance, heroism, conflict, excitement, war, suspense and surprise to write a play. Moreover, he might have thought of motivating the youth of Odisha with patriotism by writing about the glorious history of love and war. He might have been confident of winning the appreciation of the theatre audience of Odisha who is naturally inclined to spiritualism and mysticism.

The plot of *Kanchi Kaveri* is foregrounded on romantic love. Princess Padmavati, the princess of Kanchi along with her parents, King Kalabareswar and Queen Bidyullata visits Puri to pay their obeisance to Lord Jagannath during a Rath

Yatra. Purushottam Dev plays the host to the royal family. As soon as Purushottam Dev and Padmavati come across each other, they fall in love at first sight. Purushottam Dev draws a portrait of Padmavati to dote on her in her absence. He sends a proposal of marriage to the king of Kanchi. The conflict of the play begins when the King turns him down on the pretext that he is doing the mean job of a scavenger on the chariots of the Lords. Purushottam Dev's love stumbles on his humiliation. He considers his insult as an offence against Lord Jagannath and vows revenge. He swears that he will invade Kanchi, capture the princess and give her in marriage to a scavenger. Padmabati is distraught. Since the moment her eyes met the Gajapati's, she is head over heels in love with him. She has accepted Purushottam Dev as her lord. She confides in her handmaids: "Padmabati: ... The seed of love was implanted in me when I visited the King of Puri with my parents on the occasion of the Rath Yatra. When I saw him there, the seed of love in my heart germinated. I could realise that the lord my heart had become the lord of my life. ..." (Act III Scene iv)

Purushottam Dev leads an expedition to Kanchi with a vast army. Lord Jagannath and Lord Balabhadra join him as soldiers. On his way, he learns from a village milkmaid Maniki about the participation of the Lords. He is confident of his victory. He boasts of his devotion to the Lords before his courtiers.

Owing to his arrogance, Purushottam Dev is defeated in the first battle. He is full of remorse. He repents of his arrogance and wholeheartedly prays to the Lord for forgiveness. His courtier Dasa, a devotee of the Lord, conveys him the Lord's message for a second attack on Kanchi. The king of Kanchi is defeated and Padmavati is taken prisoner. Purushottam Dev entrusts the princess with his Minister and commands him to give her away to a scavenger.

The suspense of the plot deepens at this point. Both lovers pine for each other. The subjects of the kingdom of Kalinga were grief-stricken because of the King's resolve. The element of surprise occurs when the Minister presents Padmavati before the King at the next Rath Yatra while Purushottam Dev is sweeping the floors of the chariots. He pleads with him to accept Padmavati as he is doing the job of a sweeper. All the subjects, overwhelmed at the surprise turn of events, cheered the royal couple and hailed the minister for his cleverness.

The play *Kanchi Kaveri* follows the structure of the Sanskrit drama. It has a Prologue where a Sutradhara, who acts as the modern Stage Manager, introduces the play and announces its commencement. Then follows a short scene like the Shakespearean play in which two minor characters, Nata (actor) and Nati (actress) propose how the play is going to be performed on stage. Like a Sanskrit drama, the play has five acts containing structural elements: Mukha-Pratimukha-Garbha-bimarsha-nirbhana like the exposition-rising action-climax-falling action-resolution of a Shakespearean play.

The first act in two scenes presents Gajapati Purushottam Dev discussing the *modus operandi* to lead an expedition to Kanchi with his minister, jester and other members of his court to avenge his humiliation. The King was eagerly waiting for the rainy season to end so that he can invade Kanchi.

Act 2 which has only one scene depicts the milkmaid entertaining Lord Jagannath and Balabhadra with milk and butter on their way to Kanchi in the guise of warriors on their respective black and white horses. The King is overwhelmed with joy to learn this from Maniki and rewards her profusely. The place is named Manikapatana after the milkmaid.

Act 3 has five scenes. It presents Purushottam Dev to be defeated in the first battle, he is full of remorse for the defeat, the king of Kanchi is elated to learn the details of his victory from his Commander-in-Chief, Bajranada and orders a *Swayambara* (Self-selection of groom) for Padmavati. Padmavati is upset about the defeat of Kalinga and confides her distress in her maidens. She recounts how she met Purushottam Dev, how she fell in love and how he courted her as her husband. Her misery is conveyed in these words: "Today, Padmavati is like a deer hunted by a hunter in a forest. She is as helpless as a deer fleeing for life when her horns are trapped among the creepers. How can she survive?" (Act III Scene iv)

Act IV is the climax of the play. Purushottam Dev is sad and disconsolate for his defeat. He is in despair as he feels that the Lords let him down. He prays to the Lords for blessings. Dasa conveys the mandates of the Lords for a second battle. Purushottam Dev wins and Padmavati is imprisoned and brought to Puri.

Act V in three scenes depicts Purushottam Dev pining for Padmavati despite his orders to the minister to give her away in marriage to a scavenger. It depicts the minister's clever manoeuvre in offering Padmavati to the king while he is sweeping the floors of the chariots during Rath Yatra. The play ends with the union of the royal lovers.

The characterisation in the play follows a unique pattern. Both Purushottam Dev and King Kalabareswar have been portrayed with due royalty. Both of them are presented with their respective Ministers, Commanders, counsellors, warriors and priests. Court jesters are introduced to infuse humour and comic belief. While Purushottam Dev is a staunch devotee of Lord Jagannath, King Kalabareswar is a follower of Lord Ganesha. Both of them are excited in victory and miserable in defeat.

Women characters, all belonging to Kanchi, are portrayed as graceful, witty, full of understanding, sympathetic and adept in singing, all rising to the occasions as situations demand. Queen Bidyullata is portrayed as a wise queen, a loving and caring mother, concerned for the wellbeing of the princess, and devoted to Lord Ganesha. Princess Padmavati is a loving daughter, concerned for her parents, and simultaneously worried for Purushottam Dev, the lord of her heart. Two maids-in-attendance, Shasikala and Suryabala are presented as loving and caring friends like Anusuya and Priyambada of Kalidas' celebrated play *Abhijnanasakuntalam*. Bhadra, a conscientious maid of Padmavati is both a poet and a singer. She assuages distressed royal lovers with her songs and at the same time keeps the flames of love sparkling in their hearts. The only woman character of Kalinga is a milkmaid named Maniki who nourishes the famished Lords with milk, curd and butter. She is gratefully honoured by Purushottam Dev. The most important character, who is conspicuous for his sagacious wisdom and cleverness of a counsellor, is the minister.

Historical characters come alive in the play. They are humanised in the play for their dilemmas, love and care, and grief and misery. Purushottam Dev is presented more as a devotee of Lord Jagannath than as a warrior and ruler. His victory is ordained by divinity. His invasion of Kanchi is more out of his devotion to the Lords than of his love for Padmabati. Had he not commanded the Minister to give her away to a scavenger, he might have been accused of selfish interests.

Dialogues in the play are appropriate to the characters. Asides and soliloquies add a literary flavour to the play. Blank verse is used for heroic dialogues. There are seventeen songs either sung in the background or on stage. Background songs enchant the audience with melodious strains, make the audience aware of the next movement and build up the atmosphere of the play. Particularly, songs sung by Bhadra, an attendant of Padmabati, create appropriate moods of romance, excitement, pathos, misery and separation. Patriotic songs excite the heroic mood necessary for war. Ramashankar's selection of the theme appears as an anti-colonial resistance. When the Gajapati king Dibyasingh Dev was banished by the British rulers, he wrote this play to excite a feeling of belonging in the heroic people of Odisha by making them proud of their past glory. With the instance of Purushottam Dev, he wants to vindicate that offence to Lord Jagannath and his devotees can never be overlooked by the people of Odisha. Meghabarna's visit to the court of Kanchi as the ambassador of Kalinga and his depiction of the power and glory of his king vindicates the venerable position of the Gajapati.

Translation of a historical play is not an easy endeavour. One of the biggest challenges for a translator is to maintain the balance between remaining true to the original work and creating a unique piece that evokes the same responses as the original text. Even translating a single word can be cumbersome. The challenges are various: structure of the language, cultural differences, words with several meanings, compound words, missing terms, sarcasm and the like. Translating taboos and slang, similes and metaphors, using language according to the context and characters, understanding the background of the original story and its setting and translating feelings can be cited as the other difficulties.

The translator of a drama has to follow certain strategies. Before undertaking the translation of a work, he must feel confident that he has adequate knowledge of both the SL and TL. He must have a sense of the rhythm of speech patterns, particularly colloquial ones, as well as the ability to recreate the tension of dramatic situations without falsifying the playwright's intention or losing dramatic credibility within the new context.

Similarly, a playwright has poetic license to create a language of his own with a unique vocabulary of names, events and things that have great significance within the story. When such expressions are to be translated, it is a problem to maintain relevance, accuracy and context. The playwright may take recourse to wordplay as a literary device. He may employ a double entendre or spoonerism or a simple pun. The wordplay uncovers a much more serious problem in translating literature: the vast cultural gap between languages.

Ray makes a significant deviation from the popular legend. As the legend says, humiliated by the King of Kanchi when he turned down the Gajapati King's proposal of marriage to Princess Padmavati calling him a sweeper, Purushottam Dev led an expedition to Kanchi at the head of a large army to avenge his insult but he suffered a miserable defeat. He returned disappointed to Puri and prayed to Lord Jagannath to salvage the honour of a devotee like him. Following the Lord's mandate, Purushottam Dev led another invasion of Kanchi. At this time both Lord Jagannath and Lord Balabhadra accompanied the Kalinga army riding a black and a white horse respectively. Eventually, the war is won and Princess Padmavati is taken prisoner.

In Ramashankar Ray's *Conquest of Kanchi*, Lord Jagannath and Lord Balabhadra accompany the Kalinga army during the first expedition and defeat is mentioned due to Purushottam Dev's arrogance for being a devotee of the Lords. His repentance and remorse absolve him and the war is won. He has changed the historical name of the king of Kanchi, Salva Narasingh Dev to Kalabareswar. However, the incident of the Lords being entertained by the milkmaid Maniki has been adhered to.

It is not incongruous to mention the few obstacles faced by the translator while rendering the play into English. First of all, the sentence pattern in Odia is not the same as it is in English. Odia follows the subject-object-verb (S-O-V) pattern whereas English follows the subject-verb-object (S-V-O) pattern. Sometimes the verb in Odia is understood and the sense has to be followed to use the appropriate verb in English. Secondly, dramatic diction was challenging. Dialogues used in the play were informal and sometimes extremely poetic using blank verse. Dialogues using heroic blank verse, humour, sarcasm, pun, hyperbole, double entendre, and emotional outbursts needed a lot of brainstorming. Figurative languages, idiomatic expressions, culture-specific words, metaphoric terms, idioms, proverbs, phrasal verbs, interjections, onomatopoeic words, and slang in Odia do not have similar corresponding terms in English. Therefore, translation was a very challenging work. Ramashankar Ray has a rich repertoire of Sanskritised vocabulary befitting the style of a history play. Since the chief characters belong to the nobility, they use elite language. To understand the dialogues, therefore, and translate them into English needed a lot of study. Moreover, the folk idioms of the minor characters, culture-sensitive as they are, demanded a skilful study of

Odia spoken language as well as an extensive and often unsuccessful search for analogous idioms in the target language. The translator has tried to make the new English text as faithful as possible without compromising the appeal of the original text.

Dr. Bhagabata Nath
Former Reader in English

Prologue

This play of mine is not in reality a full-fledged one. Dear wise audience, a little holy water, if sprinkled over us, is enough to give us the satisfaction of a holy bath; similarly, this play will give you the pleasure of enjoying dramatic art.

SUTRADHARA: It's not necessary to go into details. There is also no need to prolong the introduction. I now greet the noble men of India present here. Today it is such a brilliant time that the intelligentsia cannot be content without a play being performed on stage. It's now the right occasion for us to do it. May god bless us for the smooth performance of the play! (*looks around. Nata enters*).

NATA: (*looking around*) Oh the wisest one! How could you bring about such a strange act? The whole place is resplendent with beauty. Spectators from all corners of the world have assembled here and glorified the place. The wealthy, the scholarly, the honourable and the noble men have taken themselves off and have been sitting here attentively. The beautiful canopy decorated with lights appears wonderful and enchants the audience. And you have kept the stage open. What is in your mind?

SUTRADHARA: Arya! Can we avail such a time? I wonder if the magnanimous audience will be able to enjoy the art. Can a liberal mind with a serious disposition and connoisseur of art be able to enjoy any other art better than this innocent pleasure? Perform on stage the newly written play, *Kanchi Kaveri* you showed me that day and had promised to stage it and entertain this august gathering.

NATA: Oh learned one, I have of course told you but it was the first dramatic work in Odia literature. It's not yet known whether the Odia language is suitable for dramatic art. How dare you perform it on stage so soon?

SUTRADHARA: What's the harm? You needn't say like that. Everything gets fit if it is polished as a polished piece of iron string produces sweet music. A play is akin to emotion. Emotion is key to it. When Odias have emotion, why shouldn't they get apt language? I know that the theme of *Kanchi Kaveri* is good. It not only possesses emotion but also contains pearls for the holy men. As a romantic person sinks into romance, an ethical person dips into ethics. This play embodies Shringara (love/beauty), Hasya (laughter), Karuna (sorrow), and Raudra (anger) *Rasas*. Moreover, it contains songs of the Lord Jagannatha's glory and beautifully describes the expedition of Shri Jagannatha and Balabhadra in support of Purushottam Dev, Padmavati's resolve, the severe oath of Purushottam Dev, the cleverness of Minister Bidyanidhi, enchanting songs of Bhadra, and uncommon devotion of Dasa. It's creditable to stage a dramatic performance on the subject of Lord Jagannatha who is visited by innumerable devotees from all over India. You need not worry. I am going to make everything ready. Try to please all those who are present here. (*Exit.*)

NATA: (*looking around*) What a good work Sutradhara engaged me in! However, a humble creature like me is encouraged by the generous crowd that has gathered here to see my performance. Today is the first staging of the Odia play. It is hard to desire that everybody will be satisfied. However, enlightened people will ignore the demerits and appreciate the merits of the play as a swan takes in the milk from a pot of milk and leaves out water. It is as unfeasible for humble people like us to entertain the learned audience with dramatic action as trying to cross the dangerous sea with a raft. Of course, I am diffident about entertaining this audience alone without my love.

(Song)
Can one cross the sea with a raft?
Can he survive waves so swift?
If a tree untimely bears a sweet fruit
Can a dirty mind ever relish it?
The lovely moon winks in the blue sky
The earth takes a dip in serene moonlight
How beautiful is lily, sweetheart
With the darling moon in the blue sky
How can lotus get such love
The sun is its paramour?
The sweetest of all is the music of the lyre
Among songbirds, the Cuckoo is no less
Dundubhi is pleasing to divine ears
My darling's voice is sweet and clear.

NATA: (*Listening to a voice from the background attentively*) Whose voice is this? Is it my sweetheart?
(*Nati enters singing…*)
(Song)
As my love is in prison
There is no joy in life,
Stung by a deadly serpent
Poison burns my heart
My peace and happiness are in ruin,
My love is a mere show,
My passion for love is in vain.
I pine for joy divine
Only end up in hell.

NATI: Aryaputra! What do you worry about?
NATA: Nothing. I was thinking of you and you too fortunately arrived here.
NATI: Is there anything important?
NATA: The task is as important as it is tough. Sutradhara has assigned the job of staging a play to me and is making all the necessary arrangements for it. An Odia play is to be staged today.
NATI: Are you going to stage the play Kanchi Kaveri today?
NATA: Yes.
NATI: It will be fine. Do it.
NATA: Can I stage the play without your help?
NATI: Aryaputra! This poor woman does not mind doing anything that pleases you and the audience.
NATA: All right then.

(Song)

Help me, O Lord, this poor man,
Entertain the loving audience
With songs in your praise.
O Lord of the universe,
ageless and formless,
O idol of wood at Neelachal abode,
Beyond mortal conception, O my Lord,
Friend of the poor, listen to my prayer,
Remove all hurdles that stare at the player,
Let the whole stage and the great hall,
Be full to the brim with 'Haribol', 'Haribol'.

NATI: Aryaputra! Come this way. See, what arrangements Sutradhara has made.

(Both exit. Curtain)

Act 1
Scene 1

King's Court, Puri

(*King Purushottam Dev, Minister Bidyanidhi, courtiers, and the court jester are seated*)

KING: Oh, Sagacious minister, when will the rainy season set in? The earth is shivering with roars of thunder and flashes of lightning. The wind is whistling. The swirling wind picks up bits of straw and sticks and sweeps the earth showing lovely scenes. Verdant nature appears comely and tender as if covered with a green cloak owing to the coolness of the season. Masses of fresh clouds cover the wide expanse of the sky. Scorched for a long time by the hot sunrays, and having a bath in the rain shower, the queen earth expresses her gratefulness to the Lord of the Universe.

    How cool it is! The water that glides along is not the water of the rains but tears of happiness rolling down. The melodious notes

	of the peacocks and peahens announce the arrival of the rainy seasons, don't they? We have been waiting for the rains as a swallow does. When will the rainy season set in?
MINISTER:	(With folded hands) Pardon my Lord, I don't know why my Lord is so anxious.
JESTER:	Eh! What a matchless minister! You cannot make out such a trivial thing. How can you apply your ingenuity to such an arduous job as the governance of the kingdom? What is the import of cleverness like ours? Ha! Ha! Ha! (Laughing) Our Lord is enchanted by the beauty of Padmavati. He should somehow visit Kanchi Kaveri. I wonder how he managed to sleep for so many days. Oh, a bachelor as he is!
KING:	Dear Acharya, you needn't say such words about me.
MINISTER:	Your Majesty, do you mean your promise in the name of Lord Jagannath? Doesn't Your Highness love Padmavati?
JESTER:	Why do you ask such a silly question to His Highness? Ask me, instead. (*Holds out a portrait.*) See, whose portrait it is. (*Hands over the portrait.*)
MINISTER:	(*takes the photo and studies it.*) Whose portrait is it? Is it of Padmavati?
JESTER:	Yes. It's of Padmavati, The bright supple elegant Padmavati with rosy lips Made up by the Lord as if in the solitude of a moonlit night, A figure with a beaming smile;

	How natural! How graceful!
	As she treads on earth, she glides like a dove With a cheerful composure; As delicate as an image of butter With a comely face as charming as a lotus in full bloom, Her beauty is as pristine as pure water, Uncommon in three worlds A damsel created by the Lord For all the gods to vie. (*All burst into a loud laughter.*)
KING:	Who says that all jesters of the world are fools?
JESTER:	Aren't I up to mark? It's ok if I am recognized as wiser than the minister. Thank me. Ha! Ha! (*Laughs*) Dear Minister, could you see how His Majesty appreciated me?
MINISTER:	My Lord! Don't you adore Padmavati? I see, Your Highness is very much keen on your oath.
KING:	Dear minister, what do you mean? Who else do I adore if not Padmavati? But gone are those days. I've dispelled those desires from my mind. I have drawn the portrait that dear Acharya has shown you now. Dear Acharya saw myself secretly drawing it during the last Rath Yatra when I beheld Padmavati for the first time.
JESTER:	See dear minister; isn't it the sign of love?
KING:	I have been pining for Padmavati in the heart of my heart. But I have discarded her from my heart since the day when the king of Kanchi called me a scavenger. Why? Doesn't

he know that the Lord I serve is the Lord of the universe, Father of all? if He feels like it, He can wipe out Kanchi from the surface of the Earth. The king of Kanchi doesn't have the sense that the Lord who is visited by all kinds of pilgrims from all corners of India, uphold the Blue Hill as Heaven and crowd it now and then can bring down his downfall and burn him to cinders. How could he call me a scavenger while I was in service of the Lord who, with His miraculous powers, has prevented the thunderous roar of the sea from being heard at the Lion Gate of His abode? Eh! The meanest of mankind, let me see how audacious you are! Guards!

GUARD: (*Coming from behind*) Your Majesty! (*Stands before the king with folded hands*)

KING: Convey my message to General Birabal to be present here.

GUARD: Yes, Your Majesty! (*Exit.*)

JESTER: His Majesty is furious.

KING: Dear Acharya, you know. Is it a trifle to be ignored?

JESTER: Your Majesty! Haven't we realised it? Isn't it serious to call a person a scavenger, who is a king and the servitor of Lord Jagannath, and who is honoured by all other kings only for his service to Lord Jagannath?

MINISTER: The king of Kanchi is a very ignoble person. That he is a king of kings is admitted. But it's not desirable that he should not be so impertinent. He should not have disregarded Lord Jagannath, the Lord of the Universe, and called the emperor names. It's unwelcome that he came along with Padmavati on a courtesy call to the emperor and called him a scavenger. If sweeping the path for the movement of the deities with sandalwood water had been a forbidden task, he should not have given his daughter in marriage to the king. It is the cause of all evil to undermine the deities and dishonour a king, and a sign of meanness too. A coconut tree is so tall but it allows other smaller plants to pass by. No, he is without wit.

BALLABHA: Dear minister, it was the incident during the procession of the Deities at the time of Rath Yatra. What did Lord Jagannath convey?

MINISTER: He would ensure victory over Kanchi during the monsoon.

BALLABHA: Yes, on the day when Dasa was released from prison, the King had the message in his dream. Monsoon has set in. Let Dasa Mahasuar be asked to pray Lord for direction. It's not a great matter for Dasa.

MINISTER: It's not necessary. Let's wait. What Lord Jagannath has conveyed will never be untrue. If it doesn't come about, we'll do that. It's only a matter of two or three days. (*General Birabal comes in, greets the King and stands before him with folded hands.*)

KING: Do you remember what the Lord commanded a few days ago?

GENERAL BIRABAL: Yes, Your Highness.

KING: Command the army to be in readiness. There should be no reason for delay when commands are issued.

GENERAL BIRABAL: Yes, Your Highness. (Exit.)
KING: Dear minister, I feel restless. As it happened today that the three chariots arrived at the Lion Gate from the abode of Ma Gundicha and the Lords ascended their seats with much ease, It seems that the Lords are not unfavourable to me. There is some mystery behind it. Dasa Mahasuar is of the same opnion. Let's wait. Let the court be adjourned.

(Curtain)

Scene 2

King's Court, Puri

(An alter for Dola ceremony in a lane. The four servitors, namely Gobardhana, Markanda, Lokanatha, and Janardana are seated.)

GOBARDHANA: Well, among us Dasa is lucky.

MARKANDA: Well, even the King honours him. What else is good luck?

GOBARDHANA: What to speak of the King! Even the Lord talks to him.

MARKANDA: See for yourself, the Lord of lords and the king of kings acknowledge Dasa. How lucky! Who among us can be so lucky as Dasa?

LOKANATHA: Oh, yes. Luck is fleeting. How is he great? How is he great if he is imprisoned? If one offers me five hundred rupees and tells me to be great like that, I'll refuse. Why? Once you are in prison, you shall be great like Dasa. You needn't praise Dasa.

MARKANDA: What do you mean? Does he lose his caste if he is imprisoned? So many people go to jail; how many of them have become as great as Dasa?

JANARDANA: (*While grinding bhang*) I feel like sage Narada and enjoy the fun.

GOBARDHANA: Try to understand Markanda. He was in prison for no fault of his. How can he help it if the King fails to understand? What to speak of Lokanatha! He always indulges in scandalising others.

LOKANATHA: What do you mean? Is it my profession only to scandalize others and you are all good people? Wasn't Dasa at fault? Why was he offering one orange once to the elder Lord and then to the younger Lord, now here and now there? Should one play pranks with the gods? Was he not at fault? Do you think that the King was insane or under a spirit while punishing Dasa?

GOBARDHANA: Do you notice Markanda? Have you understood why he was offering the same orange to several gods?

LOKANATHA: What? What is the matter?

GOBARDHANA: Why was he released from prison if there was nothing the matter with him?

LOKANATHA: Why was he released? The King imprisoned him and the King himself set him free again.

GOBARDHANA: (*mocking*) The King imprisoned him and the King himself set him free again.

	Look Markanda. I am vexed if one exaggerates anything for nothing.
LOKANATHA:	Ha! What a great man! He is vexed!
GOBARDHANA:	Why? Are you a great man?
JANARDANA:	Let the quarrel continue. Cultivator Brahmins as you are, you have no bullock guiding sticks with you, otherwise, things would have taken a different turn. I take pleasure in your squabble as sage Narada does.
MARKANDA:	Let go bro. Why do you squabble among yourselves? Why do you talk to him? (*Referring to Gobardhana*)
LOKANATHA:	Please, keep quiet. Who asks you to intervene? Our bro is coming. Yes, tell. Why was he released from prison?
GOBARDHANA:	I don't know. Think as you please. (*Sadashiva Panda arrives with a snuff box in hand.*)
SADASHIVA:	Hello, what is the matter? It is indeed a habit with the Brahmins that four Brahmins do as the four dogs do when they assemble in one place. Why do you quarrel among yourselves? (*Sniffs and sneezes.*)
MARKANDA:	I don't know. It's for nothing. It must be for something.
SADASHIVA:	If nothing is the matter, then why do you quarrel?
LOKANATHA:	Gobardhana picks up a quarrel with everybody for nothing.
GOBARDHANA:	See Markanda, I am quarrelsome but this bro Loka is innocent.

SADASHIVA:	Don't drag it further. What is the matter?
GOBARDHANA:	Can anyone give up one's bad habits? Lokanatha says that there is nobody meaner than Dasa. How can one who is sent to jail be nobler? Markanda and I were discussing Dasa's character when Lokanatha attacked us like a mad dog as if Dasa was his staunch enemy.
SADASHIVA:	Lokanatha is at fault.
LOKANATHA:	What is my fault? As if you have understood everything! Is it a judgment or a farce?
JANARDANA:	Let it continue. Even if a Brahmin has eaten to his heart's content, he won't get up.
SADASHIVA:	Hello, why are you vexed with me? Will Dasa offer me anything or do I owe you anything?
MARKANDA:	No. None of them.
SADASHIVA:	Try to understand Markanda, how will he or Dasa be of use to me? Shall I not say what I think right?
MARKANDA and GOBARDHANA:	What else!
SADASHIVA:	The King did not know that Dasa was imprisoned. It was Dasa's bad luck. But how could he get released? Didn't Lokanatha know it?
LOKANATHA:	Don't I know it?
SADASHIVA:	Do you know what He conveyed to the King in his dream when Dasa prayed to Lord Jagannath continuously for three days and three nights to save him?

LOKANATHA:	What?
SADASHIVA:	Well, why do you quarrel without knowing anything? Didn't He say, Oh King! You think of yourself to be God. You don't consider anybody other than you as God. You were mere Puria till the last noon. You became a king on my orders. Why are you so arrogant? I have not taken my food for the last three days. Release my devotee immediately. Look, Lord Jagannath Himself called Dasa a devotee.
LOKANATHA:	Yes, indeed. Why should he be proud of being a devotee? When he was moving from one deity to another with an orange, someone told him that he was summoned by the Lord; of course, he meant the King. Dasa said, "I only know one God, Lord Jagannath. I don't know any other God." Is the king a mere trifle for him?
SADASHIVA:	Why do you babble without knowing anything? Didn't the Lord say that Dasa was innocent? What is his crime? When he came with an orange to the seat of Lord Jagannath, we told him to go to Lord Balabhadra. When he moved to Lord Balabhadra, he was asked to offer it to Lord Jagannath. That was why he was moving from one God to another. It is only because of us he said, "How many gods are there?" Now, leave him alone.

LOKANATHA:	Who will believe it?
SADASHIVA:	Who will make anyone believe if one doesn't feel like it?
MARKANDA:	Well, what did the King do then?
SADASHIVA:	What else would the King do? He set Dasa free and said, "You would not have suffered so much if you had explained it to me earlier. I could only come to know about it from the Lord."
MARKANDA:	Didn't it happen on *Snana Purnima* Day?
SADASHIVA:	Yes, it happened on *Snana Purnima* Day, only twenty-five days ago. Today is the tenth day of the month.
MARKANDA:	Doesn't Lokanatha remember an incident that took place only twenty-five days ago? Why was he furious with me?
JANARDANA:	Oh, why Dasa was referred to? This *Bahuda Dasami* noon is spoilt. Would you like to take the mixed vegetable curry? It's getting late; I'm going. How do I bother if Dasa does prosper or suffer, die or survive? For my mixed vegetable curry, I don't care for Dasa. Let's go to the club. (*Rising*)
All:	Let's go. (*Rise up and about to start.*)
LOKANATHA:	I won't take the mixed vegetable curry if it is as watery as yesterday's.
JANARDANA:	Let's go, brother. I'll feed you with shit today.

(Curtain)

Scene -3

King's Bed Chamber, Puri

(*Purushottam Dev is sleeping on his bed. All of a sudden "Hail the King" is heard from the background along with the ringing of bells. The King gets up with a surprise.*)

KING: What is it? (*a guard enters.*)
GUARD: (*with folded hands*) Your Highness! There is a command from the Lord.
KING: What? Command from the Lord? Who delivered the message?
GUARD: Your Highness! Dasarathi Mahasuar is waiting for an audience. He wishes to meet Your Highness.
KING: Why does Dasarathi Mahasuar wait upon me? Let him in.
GUARD: Yes, Your Highness. (*Exit.*)
KING: (*Aside*) Why has Mahasuar called on me at such an hour of the night? Why is he in a hurry to convey the Lord's message to me?

	Let me wait.
	(*Dasarathi comes in.*)
DASA:	Hail the King!
KING:	Oh Das, come in.
DASA:	I beg your pardon, Your Highness to disturb you at such an hour.
KING:	It does not matter. What is the message from the Lord?
DASA:	Your Highness, Lord has commanded you to proceed to Kanchi Kaveri without delay.
KING:	To proceed to Kanchi Kaveri? How could the Lord remember after such a long time? Dear Dasa, I have special honour for you as the devotee of the Lord. I have complete faith in you. It has never occurred in my dream that you can utter anything meaningless. It is said that faith grows faster in grief than in happiness.
DASA:	Your Highness, I understand what you mean. But, Your Highness, you hold me in such esteem that I can't tell a lie. You know my character very well.
KING:	You needn't say anything more. Shall we start now?
DASA:	Now, before the daybreak. I ran to Your Highness as soon as I had the Lord's mandate in my dream. It's the Lord's message that you get ready immediately.
KING:	Oh, only two hours of the night remain. Guard!
	(*"Your Highness!" is heard from behind. Guard enters.*)
KING:	Convey my message to the minister and

	bring in the General, Ballabha, Jester and My Preceptor to my presence.
GUARD:	Yes, Your Highness. (*Exit.*)
KING:	Dasa, I have been really worried since I have not had the Lord's mandate for long. I have no worries now. Let us begin our expedition now. You have to accompany us too.
DASA:	What shall I do there?

The warriors shall dance in a battle frenzy
Like bloodthirsty demons in crematoria,
Battle drums in tandem shall be riotously beaten
Producing mortal refrain;
Impelled by pulsating music,
Warriors on chariots with grooms
And on elephants with mahouts
Commanders and their troops
Cavalries and foot-soldiers
Ignorant of one another
Shall be engaged in war with all their heart
Boasting of their might.
What shall a poor Brahmin do there
where mighty warriors in arms
shall be dancing to the war tune
brandishing swords and spears, bows and arrows,
and firearms as well?
Let the Kshatriyas go;
They have to fight, win the battle,
Devastate Kanchipur
And hoist the flag of victory.
Loud cheers of "Long live Odisha",
"Long live the Gajapati king of Odisha"
shall rent the air.

	Fetch Padmavati, the lovely princess
	To Your Majesty
	And fulfil your vow.
	What shall a frail Brahmin like me do there?
KING :	You are right. You don't understand that I completely depend on Lord Jagannath for this expedition. I abide by His mandate. If you don't accompany me, who will covey me the Lord's directions?
DASA:	Shall I have to go then? Well, I shall go. I am taking leave of Your Majesty now. I shall get myself ready for the journey.
KING:	You may go. Get ready soon.
DASA:	Long live the King! (*Exit.*)
KING:	Why didn't the minister and others turn up yet? The Guard has gone long ago. The night is about to end. How long shall I wait? Whose footsteps are these? Have they all come?

(*Minister, Jester, Birabal, Royal Preceptor, and Ballabha enter.*)

Have you all come?

Jester, Royal Preceptor, and BALLABHA:
Glory be to Your Majesty. (*All take their seats.*)

BIRABAL:	Glory be to Your Majesty. (*Takes his seat.*)
MINISTER:	Glory be to Your Majesty. (*Takes his seat.*) Your Majesty, why are we all called for at this hour?
KING:	Lord Jagannath has commanded that immediately, before daybreak, we have to proceed to Kanchi Kaveri.
MINISTER:	The Guard was also saying the same thing. There is nothing to worry about; we are all prepared for the expedition. We needn't delay then. Let the General soon arrange the army

	in battle order and give marching orders.
KING:	You're right. Dear General, arrange your army in battle order and let them hear the commands of Lord Jagannath: "Do or die". Go and send us the message that you are ready and we shall proceed accordingly. We'll wait for you.
BIRABAL:	Your Majesty, there is nothing to worry about it. We can vanquish the king of Kanchi without much difficulty. They have a vast army; yet they have less battle skill. Let the marching orders be issued the army will follow.
JESTER:	(*aside*) Nothing pleases a man who is already miserable! It's already a matter of taking leave from family. Who bothers about a poor Brahmin? I have been away from home since the last night. My lady might be waiting for me for some gift from the king. Had it been any other Brahmin, he could have arranged at least some fruits for his meal from the King.
KING:	Acharya, why do you seem unmindful? What do you worry about?
JESTER:	(*To himself*) Why shouldn't I tell? It's a matter of livelihood. (*To the King*) You are aware Your Majesty about this poor Brahmin. I have not tasted a good meal for several days. I thought that Your Majesty might have arranged something grand since I was called for at such hours of the night. But there have been all preparations for a war. I felt like accompanying you.
KING:	How can you be useful to me there?

The Conquest of Kanchi | 41

JESTER: Why do Your Majesty tell me so? Who will enjoy the feast when it will be arranged for our victory? (*Laughs.*)

MINISTER: What a greedy man! Acharya is thinking of his tummy when serious things are going on.

JESTER: Is that so? Dear Minister, why don't you understand who will the King confide in if I don't go? Who will recite scriptures to him? Who will understand what is in the King's mind? Can he do without a wise man?

Without the light of the sun, the earth takes many hues;

Without a jester with him, a king can never be wise.

MINISTER: Glory be to your hidden wisdom!

JESTER: The King once honoured me with the title "The Most Learned". (*Laughs.*) Your Majesty! What are your commands for me?

KING: You should go with us. Everything lies with you.

JESTER: Let me then go and take leave of my lady.

MINISTER: (*Making fun of him*) Yes, be beaten by her.

JESTER: It does not blow. It's bidding farewell. (*Exit.*)

(*The Chief Royal Astrologer Rudreswar hurriedly enters.*)

RUDRESWAR: Long live the King!

KING: Welcome, Dear Chief Foreteller. Why are you so much worried?

RUDRESWAR: Your Majesty, I learn that you are leading an expedition to Kanchi Kaveri. But it's not an auspicious time for you.

KING: Is it so? Why did the Lord so mandate?

RUDRESWAR: Please consider Your Majesty:

> On Sunday and Friday, the wise should proceed to the East,
> On Saturday and Monday to the West,
> On Saturday to the North,
> and on Wednesday to the South.
> But today is Thursday, and —
> On the nighttime of the fourth and eleventh day,
> The daytime of the eighth day of the bright fortnight
> And the full moon day as well
> The nighttime of the third and tenth day
> And the daytime of the seventh and fourth day
> Of the Dark Fortnight
> Are inauspicious.

MINISTER: It's an inopportune time!
KING: Esteemed Mishra, why do you keep quiet? Please, find out some means.
PRIEST: (*worried*) The Chief Astrologer has raised objections.
RUDRESWAR: Please consider esteemed Mishra whether my objections are valid. You will also agree with me. Baraha has detailed inauspicious moments for starting a journey.
PRIEST: These are simple things. Did you find the right moment?
RUDRESWAR: You needn't ask me about it. The King is having *Vaidhriti Yoga* which is extremely malefic for him.
PRIEST: (*shutting his ears*): Oh! *Vaidhriti Yoga*!
MINISTER: Your Majesty, it's very inauspicious.
KING: Shall I go against the mandate of the Lord?
PRIEST: Even if the world comes to an end you should abide by the Lord's wishes.

RUDRESWAR: But *Vaidhriti Yoga* cannot be ignored.
PRIEST: When the Lord has ordained the king to proceed, need we bother about any such thing? If you recite the Lord's name *Vaidhriti Yoga* can be humbled. Pray to Lord Jagannath Your Majesty and start your journey. If the Lord resides in our hearts, all inauspicious times can be auspicious and foes can be friends.
MINISTER: You are a glorious, esteemed Priest. How frail are the scriptures when the Lord prevails? (*Birabal enters.*)
BIRABAL: Your Majesty, why delay?
KING: Are you all ready?
BIRABAL: All are ready, Your Majesty. The army is on the beach in battle order waiting for Your Majesty's commands.

As the sea seems solemn without winds
The army stands too still in battle order
When Your Majesty's commands
Blows like a storm, the army will roar
Like the roaring waves of the sea.

KING: Dear minister, is there anything left for us to do?
MINISTER: No, Your Majesty. Only *Mahaprasad* is to be ready. (*Dasarathi enters.*)
DASA: Your Majesty, *Mahaprasad* has arrived. Please, get ready.
KING: It's fine. Dear General, move the army first and I am following. (*Rising.*) Let's not delay. Dear Minister, look after the administration of the state till we return.
MINISTER: You needn't worry Your Majesty.
(*Curtain*)

ACT II

SCENE I

(The Highway near Adipur. Maniki is sitting alone with her empty milk pots.)

MANIKI: *(Looking at a ring.)* How beautiful it is! How splendorous! Does a stone emit light? How does it matter to me? Great men have great affairs. One who has riches can buy five of such things. How does it matter to an empty stomach? When is he coming? I have been in a mess. I belong to a milkman's family. If there is a little delay, my mother-in-law and sister-in-law will scandalize me. I am to be blamed. Let me sit in the shade of that tree. Let's wait as long as possible. I shall not go home to be damned. *(Two soldiers enter.)*

FIRST SOLDIER: Why did the King get down from the palanquin and walk along the road?

SECOND SOLDIER: See, how good-natured he is! How noble! There are a few men as good

	as our king. A milkmaid is looking for the commander. The king has sent for her and has got down from the palanquin to meet her.
FIRST SOLDIER:	Else, the milkmaid will be frightened?
SECOND SOLDIER:	Don't you know the rustic people? If they find a simpleton, they confide in him.
FIRST SOLDIER:	Unless a man is noble, he cannot occupy such a position. That woman who you were laughing at …
SECOND SOLDIER:	Be quiet, the King is coming. Let's now leave this place.
	(*Soldiers exit. Purushottam Dev and Dasa enter.*)
KING:	did you notice how clever is the milkmaid?
DASA:	This village looks impoverished but the woman has put on heavy ornaments.
KING:	This is a highway marketplace, a place for trading activities. She might be the daughter of a well-to-do milkman. Let's see. (*Birabal and Jester enter along with Maniki carrying her basket.*) What is the matter?
JESTER:	Your Majesty, a hunter was passing through a forest with a net. He hoped to trap a pair of parrots for the king as a gift. Wonderfully, to the king's god fortune, he trapped a damsel, a paragon of beauty with a face as bright as the spotless moon, gracefully

attired and seductively enchanting. The poets have popularly portrayed a damsel as one who has a heavy gait like the elephant's, with glowing red lips, a slim neck like a peacock's, a hooked nose like a parrot's, with a slim waist like a lion's, with agile eyes like a doe's, with a sweet voice like the cuckoo's, with seductive eyelashes that resemble the bow and arrow of Cupid, with teeth glistening like *Kunda* flower, with arms slender as the stem of a lotus flower, her feet being as tender as the lotus petals, with a bright face like the full moon and her laughter is bewitching. Poets have depicted beautiful women to the extent of boredom. You can compare, Your Majesty, the damsel's stylish attire with her grace.

KING: Dear Acharya, are you trying to be a poet? Didn't the hunter disappear with the damsel?

JESTER: Need you say like this, Your Majesty? It is said that two persons are born for each other. You know, Your Majesty, that I am a poet. Why should I try to be a poet? Of course, if one comes across a charming blooming bud of matchless beauty swinging in the soft breeze, grown on a tree of imagination, a dullard shall become a poet. You too are a poet otherwise you

	wouldn't be fascinated by her. You can test it: gold glistens if purged by fire. You are fire and she is gold; you can check whether she is beautiful.
KING:	Good; you are the wisest guy.
JESTER:	(*Amused.*)
The KING:	What is the matter now?
MANIKI:	(*Piteously.*) Your Majesty, two men drank all my milk and curd and went away. When I asked for payment, they told me that their commander was following them and asked me to collect my dues from them.
KING:	Took milk and curd without payment? How did you give them without payment? Who dared to do it in our rule? Impossible!
MANIKI:	it's not untrue, Your Majesty. Please look at this ring. (*Hands over a ring.*)
KING:	it's a very attractive precious ring. What does it mean? Is it yours? Who did you get it from?
MANIKI:	We are destitute, Your Majesty. Where can we get it? They gave me this ring as proof lest the commander should not believe me. They told me to keep this ring with me and exchange it for money.
DASA:	(*Took the ring from the King and peered at it.*) Your Majesty, it looks like the ring of Lord Balabhadra.
KING:	What? Is it the ring of Lord Balabhadra? Are you crazy?

JESTER:	Dasa is out of his mind, Your Majesty. Your wit has become blunt. Sharpen it quickly or exchange it with somebody else's.
KING:	Your mind is sharp; exchange it with him.
JESTER:	If Your Majesty commands me so. I have already tried but Dasa's mind has already been hacked.
DASA:	(*aside*) The Lord has told me to come today. He might have taken her milk and curd. I need not tell it to His Majesty now. Let it be proved. (*To the King*) Please see Your Majesty, it must be Lord Balabhadra's ring. (*To Maniki*) Hello, how do they, who enjoyed your milk and curd, look like?
MANIKI:	Sir, one of them was dark and the other was white-complexioned. They fed their horses and their grooms with whatever was left. When I asked them for payment, the dark one refused and the White one gave me this ring. I am in deep trouble, sir; kindly help me. (*Wipes her tears with the end of her sari.*)
DASA:	Be quiet. You needn't worry. You are very fortunate. Please see Your Majesty, firstly, such a precious ring is rare; secondly, it's the same ring. Please mark again that one of those two who ate her milk and curd was

The Conquest of Kanchi | **49**

	dark and the other white. The dark one is a troublemaker; He might have refused to pay but the white one is straightforward; He had left the ring with her.
KING:	How strange! Aren't there any human beings like them?
DASA:	There is one more thing for you, Your Majesty, to consider. (*To Maniki*) Hello, which of them is the elder one?
MANIKI:	The fair complexioned.
DASA:	Were they riding horses?
MANIKI:	The fair one had a dark horse and the dark one had a white horse. Please pay my dues, Sir.
DASA:	Wait, you will get four times what is your due. (*To the King*) Please consider, Your Majesty. (*To Maniki*) Did they tell you anything about their identity? Their parents' name or anything else?
MANIKI:	No, Sir. The younger one was fostered by a woman named Yashoda. He used to milk the cows and buffaloes there. I don't know anything more about them. Yes, one of their grooms was Ankara and the other was Urdhava.
KING:	Is it a dream?
JESTER:	Birabal, am I asleep or awake? What is this?
DASA:	Now, Your Majesty, give up your doubts,

	Give up all your fears and anxieties, it's not a dream,

Give up all your fears and anxieties, it's not a dream,
God's ways are incomprehensible;
Who can comprehend the fine web of illusion woven by the Lord of gods,
Whose very name is enough to make the Heaven tremble,
Whose commands are obeyed even by Lord Brahma and Lord Shiva?
Who so powerful as to get through His web of illusion,
Which is much finer than that of the spider?
He is not a mere human being, Your Majesty.
He must be the Lord of Radhika and the beloved of the gods.
(*To Maniki*) When did you see them?

MANIKI: A little while ago. They disappeared before long.

KING: How strange!

DASA: Did they tell you anything about where they were going?

MANIKI: They said that they were going to Kanchi to take part in the battle.

KING: What is it, dear Dasa?
Is Lord Jagannath along with Brother Lord Balabhadra
Taking so much pains to proceed to Kanchi
To take part in the battle to fulfil my vow?
I can now realise myself too well.

Is there anyone on earth a greater devotee than me
Who is so reverently immersed in devotion to God?
There is no one more fortunate than he
For whom the gods take pains to help;
He is very much revered in the society.
Am I not more blessed than the being who cannot easily avail a glimpse of the Lord,
however hard he mediates on Him living an austere life in a graveyard renouncing everything
even though he has turned into a skeleton;
than Lord Brahma,
who waits on the Lord for a glimpse so long
that he gets an aching throat while singing his hymns?
Who is as blessed as I am?
(*To Dasa*) Ask the milkmaid, Dasa, what she needs.
I'll never turn down her prayer.

JESTER: Glory be to Your Majesty; the Lord's ways are unintelligible.

DASA: Please understand Your Majesty, why the Lord commanded you to pay a visit to Lord Durga Madhab and start your expedition. (*To*

	Maniki) What do you need, Maniki? See, the Lords, both Jagannath and Balabhadra, ate milk and curd from your baskets. Who is more fortunate than you?
MANIKI:	(*Aside*) How unfortunate I am! I could not recognize the Lords. (*To Dasa*) Sir, if the Lords have taken milk and curd from me, I don't need anything. I wish everybody knew it.
KING:	Look Dasa, how clever Maniki is! you are very fortunate. Whose daughter are you?
MANIKI:	Brusha Behera's.
KING:	Brushabha ... Brushabhanu Behera's? Well, Dasa, tell Maniki that the area he covers by walking now shall belong to her. A village shall be set up here after her name. it will be named Manikipatana and it will be free from revenue tax. Maniki and her heirs shall enjoy it. I am just giving it to her on paper and later, a brass plate record will be issued. I am leaving. Settle everything and come after me. (*A milkman enters and prostates before the King. Maniki withdraws a little in her father's honour.*)
KING:	Who are you? Get up.
BRUSHABHA:	I am Brushabha Behera. When I heard that Your Majesty had arrived, I left my responsibilities to others and came before you. Here are

	Maniki's mother and mother-in-law. They have come to pay their homage to you.
KING:	Call them. (*Two women enter an aarti plate, holy water, sandalwood paste and flowers.*)
BRUSHABHA:	Come in (*The King takes off his shoes and stretches his right foot. The women did arati to honour the king. They ululated. Sounds of conch shells blowing are heard from the background.*)
KING:	Go and call all women. Perform an inauguration ceremony for Maniki and offer prayers to Lord Jagannath. (*The two women and Maniki exit.*) Brushabhanu, your wishes are fulfilled now. Lord Jagannath and Lord Balabhadra have enjoyed milk and curd from your daughter. You will hear about it in detail later. Come with me now. You will get a written order from me. (*The King along with* Jester, Birabal *and* Brushabha *exit.*)
DASA:	(*Aside*) The King has steadfast devotion to the Lord. I don't feel like staying in any other kingdom. The King is as wise as learned and devoted as well as generous. He will never hesitate to do any noble deed. He is ever willing for anything and never undermines anybody. However, a splendid landmark has been set up. All these are the Lord's

	play. (*Brushabha enters with four other milkmen and an official deed.*) Did you get the official order?
BRUSHABHA:	Yes, Sir.
DASA:	Let me see. (*Takes it from Brushabha.*) Good. Let's go and spot the area to set up a village.
ALL MILKMEN:	Please wait, Sir. Let's have a game of *Naudi* in the name of Madhoi (Lord Krishna). Let the women assemble here. Let this game continue for all ages. Krishna is ours for all ages. (*The game of Naudi starts. Blowing of conch shells and ululating women is heard at intervals.*)
	(Song)
	Why do you stop us, oh Kanha?
	Who can pay the ferry ghat charge in Kansa's reign, oh Kanha?
	My sister-in-law and mother-in-law are wicked, oh Kanha?
DASA:	Well, stop. We have a hurry. You can pay to your heart's content after the inauguration ceremony is over. (*All exit.*)
	(*Curtain*)

(*Song from background*)
Let's chant the name of Sri Jagannath in one voice;
Let there be victory in the battle of Kanchi;
Let the desire of the Devotee be fulfilled;
Let all Gandharvas and Nymphs sing in one voice;
Let all the devotees of the world sing the glory of the Lord.

ACT III

SCENE I

(The Kingdom of Kanchi. The Royal groove. Padmavati is lying down in the groove as if in the pangs of separation. Shasikala and Suryabala are fanning her.)

SHASIKALA:	Oh! The Princess has fallen asleep after several days.
SURYABALA:	See dear friend, how ashy pale the beautiful princess has become! Ah! Being a princess, she should have been moving about with pride but she has been reduced to a mere skeleton being burnt up in sorrow. *(wipes out her tears with the end of her sari.)*
SHASIKALA:	Dear friend, the wearer knows where the shoe pinches. She only knows what troubles her mind. We can only know her external troubles. She only knows what in her mind is. Even if we use lotus leaves and khuskhus roots to fan her, she feels the wind hot. Even if the Siris flower is spread

on her bed, she feels as if sleeping on a bed of thorns. Therefore, it is said:
Pangs of separation hurts her soul, How can she make out good or evil? Even though His Majesty feels sad for her and is sometimes vexed with her, she has lost her appetite for food. She has given up food and water, sleeping, walking or sitting. *(feeling the body of the Princess.)* Touch her body and feel how hot it is! She behaves as if she has gone mad. Ah! How long will she survive, if she continues like this? *(Sheds tears.)*

SURYABALA: *(feeling the body of the Princess.)* Isn't His Majesty aware why the Princess is remorseful; why she is absentminded? Why doesn't he take steps for any remedy for her ailment?

SHASIKALA: Are you crazy? Do you know how four physicians attend to her twice a day and prescribe medicines for her? How can physicians help if one's mind and heart are bitten by bugs? He can only check the pulse and prescribe a mixture of medicine to drink and an oil for massage

SURYABALA: Well dear, what shall we do if we are appointed as physicians?

SHASIKALA: What makes you laugh? What you said is right. We shall immediately bring the king of Odisha. Only a

	woman can look after a woman's ailment. The menfolk will somehow collect their dues. Our mind is our greatest physician.
SURYABALA:	Why don't the parents understand their child's heart?
SHASIKALA:	There lies the trouble. You know that our king has condemned the Gajapati King as a sweeper.
SURYABALA:	No, the Princess should not pine for him. It is said
	Water is to be taken after it is filtered, Money is accepted after it is counted, A relationship is made after having scanned.
	The Princess should understand it. Another candidate shall be selected. What is there to be worried about?
SHASIKALA:	Can anyone outdo the Princess in cleverness? No sooner did she come across the Gajapati King than she dedicated herself to him. Where is the need for filtering, counting or scanning? As soon as she beheld him, she was lost. Did she leave any scope for scanning?
SURYABALA:	A hasty decision is light.
SHASIKALA:	Why do you say so? Can you say when a thing is light? It is said:
	A young maiden is light in all matters, But heavy in the affair of shyness.
	Don't you know it? Haven't you

	realised it when you had your first love?
SURYABALA:	We are no match for a princess.
SHASIKALA:	Is there any difference between you and the princess in affairs of love? All are equal in this regard. It is said that love is blind.
SURYABALA:	When our King called him a sweeper, he said that he would marry the Princess to a sweeper. One who said like this, how can the Princess …
SHASIKALA:	(*gesturing*) Be quiet. You needn't repeat it here. It will be like setting the sea on fire. We needn't bother about it. But I am heartbroken to see all this.
SURYABALA:	Dear pal, I feel for her. Who can we tell what is there in the destiny of the Princess? However, something undesirable might happen.
SHASIKALA:	Is there any doubt about it? Is there anything desirable going to happen when parents insist that they will not give their daughter in marriage to the Gajapati King and the daughter is not willing to marry anybody else? I don't find anything desirable to happen. Something of great import might happen. Let it go, dear friend. Let's not talk about it any longer. My heart aches. I feel like crying when I glance at the Princess. (*Heaves a sigh.*) Oh God! Everything depends on you.

SURYABALA:	Please, save the miserable Princess. (*Wiping her tears from Shasikala's eyes with the end of her sari*) Don't cry. Who will console the Princess if you cry? The Princess has fallen asleep a little today. Fan her a little. If she sleeps for a while, she will come round. (*Fans with the chamar fan.*)
SHASIKALA:	(*heaves a sigh.*) Oh, yes. (*fans with the chamar fan.*)
PADMAVATI:	(*with a feeble voice*) Ah! Who? Is it Shasi? Dear Suryi, my dear sister, my bosom friend, fan me like that. May you live long!
SHASIKALA:	Dear Sister, how can we live if you are miserable? We are happy if you are happy. If you are happy, we would like to live for ages.
PADMAVATI:	My darling, I am destined to suffer. (*falls asleep again*) (*Saramali enters.*)
SURYABALA:	Hi! Sari, why are you here?
SARAMALI:	Mother has come.
SURYABALA:	Who? Bhadra? Sister, Bhadra has come. Shall we invite her?
PADMAVATI:	Bhadra? My life! Call the mother.
SURYABALA:	Go and call her in. (*Saramali exits.*)
SHASIKALA:	Pal, it's a great quality of Bhadra … however sad you are …. What enchanting ways she has…
SURYABALA:	True. I sometimes feel like that. (*Bhadra enters with a violin and a garland of rosary.*)

SHASIKALA:	(*laughing*) What has happened today? Why are you beaming with laughter?
BHADRA:	(*posturing for a song*) It is he, Banamali, the new keeper of wild blossoms, Decked with a peacock feather, plays on his flute in a unique pose under the *Kadamba* tree; knows the mind, steals the heart romances in a grove with darling Radhika
SHASIKALA:	Eh! Singing in a romantic vein!
SURYABALA:	(*mocking*) Might have been in touch with a romantic monk!
SHASIKALA:	Who is that romantic monk?
BHADRA:	One who is head over heels in love with me.
SHASIKALA:	(*Laughing loudly*) What about you?
BHADRA:	Waiting for a long time My dark lover doesn't appear, My new love has waited so long My fair colour has been darker.
SHASIKALA:	Very good! What happened then?
BHADRA:	All her make up is in vain The lover doesn't appear, The romantic lover, the cunning lover, As shameless as ever. The darling is waiting in the grove Krishna has been unfair, A tall talker is he in the world, What a playful lover! The sweet notes of his flute

	All the night she cannot hear,
	The night is over, where's the lover?
	All his words are on water.
	Her soul is bleeding,
	Her head is reeling,
	The darling pines for the lover;
	She is in tears, life is bitter,
	Her mind is nowhere.
SHASIKALA:	Then?
BHADRA:	Darling Radhika sulks in silence,
	With such a heavy heart;
	Can swift wind move a hill
	As weighty as her heart?
	Clueless Mohan, the silent lover,
	Took her bonny feet in hand;
	Put them on his lowered head,
	Thus, all his love is conveyed.
SURYABALA:	Will it be the same in this case?
BHADRA:	Exactly like that. Let the lover come with his flute. (*sits near Padmavati's head and sings.*)
	(*Song*)
	Give up, darling, all your rancour,
	It is all for nothing;
	Why are you so downcast,
	Why are you so withered?
	Why are your eyes so moist,
	as a lotus with dewy bead?
PADMAVATI:	Maa Bhadra, nothing but your enchantment can soothe this grief-stricken heart of mine. Please take a little pain for this humble soul.
BHADRA:	It's no pain for me. (*continues the song*)

	I'll pluck flowers from Heaven,
	I'll plunder Lord's Paradise,
	If you so like. If you so wish.
	My self and soul are all yours,
	You make my life glorious.
	How do you feel now, Padma?
PADMAVATI:	Why do you put this question to me?
	(*Closes her eyes.*)
BHADRA:	Don't you feel good?
SHASIKALA:	Dear Bhadra, what is fine and good about her? Don't you see her condition? She is not like the Padmavati of earlier days.
BHADRA:	Ah! How burnt up my darling is! Dear Sashi,
	The sea of beauty is consumed by fire,
	Her heart is broken for the Divine ire.
	(*Heaves a deep sigh and holds the hands of Padmavati.*)
	Oh, my virtuous one! How could you put up with so much pain? Be calm. Leave everything to the Lord. You shouldn't care for such needless agony.
	(*Song*)
	Take heart, my darling.
	My heart aches for you,
	My patience gives way.
	So much have we to suffer,
	There's no end to misery;
	Keep it in mind what I say
	No one can end your misery.

	How much you love him
	Your darling doesn't know.
	Can he ignore it if he knows
	How much do you love him?
	How can he ignore
	When I'll let him know
	How much do you adore?
PADMAVATI:	Oh, dear Bhadra, may I behold your lovely face forever! May your melodious voice please my ears and soothe my heart for good!
BHADRA:	Dear Padma, I wish I would sit with you for all ages and sing your glory. Suryi, where is Saramali going so hurriedly? *(Saramali enters.)* Why are you in such a hurry?
SARAMALI:	Her Majesty has sent for the Princess.
BHADRA:	Darling, get up. You are called for.
PADMAVATI:	Shasi, let's go. (*Rises slowly.*)

(*Curtain*)

SCENE II

(The Courtroom of Kanchi. King Kalabareswara, Minister Dhira Prajna, and courtiers are seated.)

KING: Dear minister, we needn't delay. Don't make mistakes in sending invitation cards to all important kings.

MINISTER: Everything is ready. We have been waiting for the orders of Your Majesty.

KING: Shall we invite all the kings except the king of Odisha?

KING: (*Being furious*) Never utter that sweeper's name in my holy place. Our Padmavati is neither ugly nor destitute.

MINISTER: Yes, Your Majesty. Will the *Swayamvara* ceremony be held on the coming Full Moon Day? After one month from today?

KING: Yes, just after thirty days from today. Issue orders to the Event Manager to get the stage and altar and all decorations ready. Check that all arrangements are complete four days before the event. Everything must be

	ready on the appointed day. All the rest sheds must be completed in the Sarasota area. Ask the *karji* to get all the lighted pillars and firecrackers ready. All the residents of the capital should get the necessary provisions. Announcements should be made that all the subjects should make merry for at least a week. Make arrangements for distributing food and dress to the poor and the needy.
MINISTER:	Yes, Your Majesty. (*the guard enters.*)
GUARD:	(*with folded hands*) Your Majesty, a messenger from Odisha is waiting at the gate for an audience.
KING:	(*in surprise*) A messenger from Odisha?
GUARD:	Yes, Your Majesty.
KING:	Let him in. (*the guard exits.*) Dear Minister, can you think of the purpose of his visit?
MINISTER:	Your Majesty, perhaps the intention is not good. (*the messenger comes in, bows and stands before the king with folded hands.*)
MINISTER:	What is your name?
MESSENGER:	Meghabarna.
MINISTER:	What is the purpose of your visit?
MESSENGER:	To convey the message of the king of Odisha.
KING:	The king of Kanchi Kaveri has nothing to do with the king of Odisha. Purushottam Dev comes from a

	milkman in the royal palace. He has not honoured his position as a king and acts as a sweeper. Even though he is a king, the king of Kanchi is not willing to be on friendly terms with him.
MESSENGER:	Your Majesty, you have had the first blow of an axe on that tree of friendship. When God wills to restore the previous status, something serious will take place because the attacker will not easily accede.
KING:	If the tree itself is old and full of thorns, it invites the attacker. Your king is a beast and his conduct is beastly.
MESSENGER:	Such senseless scandalisation of Your Majesty is a misuse of your nobility.
KING:	(*Being furious*) Who are you, messenger? How dare you answer me back at my royal court? Can you imagine what your fate shall be for your insolence? You will be smashed as a mosquito? If you have any message to deliver, do it with due honour to the royal court.
MESSENGER:	Please be calm, Your Majesty. A humble messenger without wisdom like me has not made any blunder. I have only said if you call our king names, all our king's noble qualities are disregarded here.
KING:	That is enough for a crime. That

	is enough dishonour. You are yet to realise that I am the ruler of this territory. Therefore, you underestimated my wisdom and accused me of ignoring his good qualities. Have you come here to teach me good etiquette? You have to pay dearly for it. Well, tell me what you want to say. You are given full liberty.
MESSENGER:	(*aside*) This king is very adamant; otherwise dare he condemn Lord Jagannath? I am sure he must imprison me and would not let me off. Here statesmanship won't do. Why shouldn't I speak straight? (*To the King*) Your Majesty, if you continue to maintain your earlier stance and take me amiss, this humble messenger is prepared for that. As I have accepted the role of an ambassador, I have taken such an eventuality for granted. An ambassador is a king's mouthpiece and his vehicle as well. His Majesty's command is his duty. I am a dimwit, you are the king of kings. Will Your Majesty please consider to relate why you condemn the king of Odisha as a sweeper? The king of Odisha is no less in

wealth or honour. He is so fortunate in this world that the Lord of the Universe gladly enjoys his devotion and service. One who serves the noble being is also renowned on earth. Doesn't the noblest blossom attain divinity? If all were fortunate, why should there be any difference between great or small? The king of Odisha is great. He is destined to be so. It's not an ordinary thing. I also agree with Your Majesty that he does act as a sweeper. It is his right as the King. His humility adds to his glory. May Your Majesty elucidate it!

It is the law of nature:
He, who is engrossed in worldly pleasures,
Whose heart is consumed by the fire of materialism,
 Boasts of himself as the greatest.
He, whose heart is like the sea of wisdom,
Where slow breeze blows
And ripples of sagacity rise in his heart,
is as calm as the Pacific Ocean.
He deems himself a tiny insect in human society.
He is also like the tiniest insect before the Lord.
Why should he feel ashamed

If he is less than a sweeper before his Lord?
How can humbleness be the cause of shame?
How beautiful a tree looks
When laden with fruits it bends down!
Can a tree bereft of fruits be like it?
A nitwit moves like a crazy guy
Imparting knowledge like a jackal
Who once taught his folk
That a tail is an unnecessary burden
A cause of sorrow,
A hindrance while running.
It's the law of nature,
A wise man honours the wise.
He who loves eating tells the quality of food.
People who live by the river love it.
But for a desert dweller,
a river spoils the beauty of the landscape.
Your Majesty has undermined Lord Jagannath
And called the king a sweeper
Which a sweeper dare not say.
If you repent of it, prostrate before the Lord,
You will be redeemed of your sins,
If with sincere devotion
You beg His excuse for a thousand times;
Or else the message I have for you will certainly prevail.

	Our king's oath is as firm as a mountain; He is advancing with a vast army, To avenge the humiliation you meted out to him, By refusing his proposal of marriage with your daughter. My Lord will conquer the kingdom of Kanchi, Reduce you to a scavenger And surrender Padmavati to a scavenger.
KING:	A scavenger! Damn you! How dare you talk such nonsense? Don't you know that the king of Kanchi can kick the heads of thousands like you? Your king's foul demeanour has made you arrogant. You are like the attendant spirit of Lord Yama, the king of Death. Minister, imprison him.
MINISTER:	It is your good fortune, messenger that our king is generous enough to spare your life.
MESSENGER:	I don't mind. I have dedicated my life to the job of an ambassador. I don't hesitate to suffer its consequences. But, what I have said will certainly come true.
KING:	Hold your tongue. Minister, send him to prison.
MINISTER:	(*with folded hands*) Your Majesty, I have a humble submission. This is

	a goddamn messenger. He cannot be imprisoned. It's like making our hands dirty by killing an obnoxious mole.
A hunter hunts a dear in the forest
To satisfy his hunger with honour
But who can say   by which hole a jackal lurks
Waiting for his prey?
Does a lion ever hunt a mouse in the forest?
It's honourable to tackle an equal.
Let the king of Odisha come.
He will himself see our prowess.
He will flee for his life from the scorching sun.
He will return of his own accord
As if hurled into hell when humbled by us.
A small fry, trounced by a mighty foe!
KING:	(*angrily*) Be quiet. Does he still shrivel for his offence?
Are you confounded by fear?
Are you frightened by the words of the messenger?
Didn't he humiliate me in my court?
If you love your life,
put the messenger under chains.
Bind his hand and feet, throw him into the prison,
Or else he will be put under the butcher's sword.

MINISTER:	Yes, Your Majesty. Guard! (*from background*) Yes, Your Majesty. (*the guard enters.*)
MINISTER:	Secure him safely and entrust him with the Prison-in-Charge. Let him be kept under chains until further orders.
GUARD:	Yes, Your Majesty. (*The guard exits with the prisoner safely secured.*)
KING:	Dear minister, put all other business on hold. Issue orders to the Commander-in-Chief to complete all arrangements and get ready for the war within two days. You are in complete charge. everything should be taken care of. The court is adjourned.

(*Curtain*)

SCENE III

(The Royal Bedroom in Lady's apartment. Queen Bidulatta is in bed. Padmavati is standing before her with head downcast.)

QUEEN: You must not object to what your mother says. How do you defy me? I see that you have not been in a good disposition since we returned from Sreekshetra. You are reducing day by day. Your colour has faded. Your veins are visible. Your ribs can be counted. Why? Why do you tell me that you won't marry? Aren't you of marriageable age? Why don't you reveal what is in your mind? All the physicians are not effective but your condition doesn't improve. Tell me which king you like to marry. Tell his name, my darling, I'll give you in marriage to that king. Do tell me, my dear.

PADMAVATI: *(aside)* Oh, My God! Were it so easy, why does a luckless maid like me suffer? *(To the queen)* Maa! I don't feel like marrying now. Why do you worry about me?

QUEEN:	Are you repeating the same thing? You suffer bodily for your emotional turmoil. How long can you hide it from me? Who told you to marry none other than the king of Odisha? Are you wiser than your parents? What qualities does the king of Odisha have to deserve a paragon of beauty like you? Other kings are more deserving than him to vie for you. Why do you insist on him? Does a sweeper who does sweeping before lakhs of people deserve your hand in wedlock?
PADMAVATI:	Maa! It is better to know about me only from me. Why do pay heed to the cock and bull story about me from anyone else? I don't feel like marrying now. Why do you condemn an innocent person? (*The King enters all of a sudden and the Queen gets up and respectfully keeps standing.*)
KING:	My Dear! What is the issue at hand?
QUEEN:	Why do you invite the kings when Padmavati is not willing to marry despite my best efforts to convince her? You need not mind about it. What is in her mind is not clear. Are all the kings invited?
PADMAVATI:	(*aside*) Oh, my God! Shall I lose my honour? Oh, Lord! I have a small prayer. Please save me from dishonour.

KING:	(*thoughtfully*) No.
PADMAVATI:	(*aside*) What a relief! I need not fear. There is nothing so far to be disappointed about.
QUEEN:	Why do you seem worried?
KING:	No, what should I worry about? We have been discussing that today. A new problem has cropped up.
QUEEN:	(*apprehensively*) What kind of problem?
KING:	The king of Odisha is coming to attack us.
QUEEN:	(*being frightened*) To attack us? Why? What shall be done now?
PADMAVATI:	(*aside*) Oh God! Is it for me that my Lord has to fight? My Lord, I am now convinced that you have not forgotten me. But it's my humble prayer before you to spare my parents.
KING:	Didn't I call him a sweeper? That is why he is coming to reduce me to a sweeper, and as I have refused to give Padmavati in marriage to him, he will marry her to a sweeper. How dare he?
QUEEN:	(*bites her tongue in fear*) What?
KING:	Why do you fear, darling? What can he do? As arrogantly as he comes, so shamefully he will go back.
QUEEN:	Who has brought this news?
KING:	A messenger has come.
QUEEN:	Where is he now?
KING:	In the prison. He used very harsh words. So, I have put him in the prison.
QUEEN:	(*pathetically*) I am worried. (*Taking*

PADMAVATI:	*Padmavati into her embrace and kissing her affectionately*) Oh God! Save us from this disaster. Let us not be humiliated! (*shedding tears, aside*) Oh God! Let Your wish prevail. I have no other refuge but you.
QUEEN:	(*wipes her and Padmavati's tears with the end of her sari.*)
KING:	Padmavati is upset if you are restless. She has been reduced to a skeleton. You should not trouble her. Be calm. I feel restless if Padma is unhappy. Don't make her cry. Take heart. You can understand Padma. Don't cry. My darling, be quiet.
QUEEN:	(*while shedding tears*) Oh, the apple of my eye! I have put up with a lot of pain for you. If you live happily in future, I'll tell you everything that is in my mind and both of us will cry our hearts out. I have not been in myself since I conceived you. Oh, my God! (*cries*)
KING:	I should conduct yourself like this now. Worship Lord Ganesha and mitigate all your sorrows. Why do you bother about the fears for the king of Odisha? (*A song from the background accompanied by violin.*) Oh, my dear wise pal! Who are you inclined to?

	Who has caused you so much sorrow? Your luminous face, as bright as the Full Moon, has waned, And all your happiness has withered. Oh, my darling! My happiness lies In thy happiness.
KING:	Is Bhadra coming?
QUEEN:	Who else is as mad as she? She can make anybody as mirthful as she is. (*Bhadra enters.*)
KING:	Bhadra has come. Everything will be set right. Let all the women folk pray to Lord Ganesha for our victory in the war. I am leaving now. Very soon orders will be issued for the subjects of the city to decorate their houses and offer their prayers. (*Exit.*)
QUEEN:	Dear Bhadra, fetch the priest immediately. Assemble all the married women of the palace in one place.
BHADRA:	(*Bows.*) I am leaving. Radha walks to the grove; who can prevent her? (*Slowly walking out.*)
QUEEN:	Padma, why are you so miserable? Let's worship Lord Ganesha. Who can harm us when he is for us? Let's go and make all the arrangements. (*The Queen along with Padmavati exit.*)
BHADRA:	Alas! How much sorrow my darling shall put up with? I am at a loss with her sorrow. (*Sits down on a chair. A song from the background accompanied by violin.*)

Oh, my dear and wise pal!
Who are you inclined to?
Who has caused you so much sorrow?
Your luminous face,
as bright as the Full Moon, has waned,
And all your happiness has withered.
Oh, my darling! My happiness lies
In thy happiness.
You dote on him night and day
But he has wiped you off his mind.
Tender in mind as she is,
She is heartbroken and has gone mad.
Oh, my soft-spoken darling!
You are swept by the current of
sorrows of the world.
One sea of sorrow follows another,
If you are fated to suffer,
You must suffer, oh my dear!
Oh, a devoted paramour!
It is the divine order.
It's only God, our ultimate hope,
Redeemer of sorrow,
He who knows our heart's desire
Will relieve us of our sorrow.
He loves His devotees,
a friend of the poor,
Keep it in mind, oh my dear!
Let me go. Her Majesty will visit
Lord Ganesha alone if I am late.
(*Curtain*)

SCENE IV

(The Temple of Lord Ganesha. The Royal Priest is seated by the altar. All necessary things for the Lord's worship are ready. The Queen, the women folk of the city, Padmavati, both her companions and Bhadra are present.)

QUEEN: Are there any women left?
BHADRA: No, Your Majesty. (*singing*)
　　　　　When notes of the flute are heard,
　　　　　No one delays.
QUEEN: Well, let the rituals begin, sir.
PRIEST: For whom will the Puja be done?
QUEEN: The king of Odisha is launching a war against us to capture Padmavati and give her in marriage to a sweeper. My humble prayer before the lotus feet of Lord Ganesh is that my daughter be the queen of the illustrious king and live happily ever after. (*Bows down with devotion.*)
　　　　　(*Suddenly a flower falls from the head of Lord Ganesha.*)
PRIEST: Be it so. Your Puja is complete.
QUEEN: Lord Ganesh is pleased with me. The rest is Padmavati's destiny. I need not worry.

BHADRA: *(The rituals are duly complete with ululating of women, sounds of conch shells and tinkling of bells.)*
(plays on the violin and sings)
(Song)
In Kanchipur flow the waves of happiness
At the root of jubilation is Lord Ganesh.
Bells tinkle, conch shells blown,
Pipes are played, ululate women,
Drums are beaten in melodious strain
All sing in one voice,
The glory of Lord Ganesh.

All houses in Kanchipur
Are decorated with flowers
Auspicious notes fill all corners
All in Kanchipur merrily rejoice.

All women assemble in one place,
Wish all happiness
To their king, queen and princess.

(Queen prostrates and others follow her.)

PRIEST: Your majesty, it is evident from the signs that Lord Ganesha is pleased and there is apprehension for anything ominous. It's all auspicious. Please accept the vermilion offering. Let me take your leave. *(offers flowers and vermilion to Queen and exits.)*

QUEEN:	(*puts vermilion mark on the forehead of all married women*) Bless Padma to be an empress and to live her life happily. (*All women bow their heads.*) Padma, shall we go now?
PADMAVATI:	Please, go ahead of me. I'm following you with my friends and Bhadra.
QUEEN:	Come back soon. (*Queen and all women exit.*)
PADMAVATI:	(*To Bhadra*) As long as you are with me, I am not frightened even by the fall of thunder. Your melodious song removes all my worries and anxieties.
BHADRA:	Dear Padma! It's all for your grace. You have nurtured my life. How can I forget it even for a while? I have devoted my life to your happiness. Why are you exaggerating my services for you?
	(*Song*)
	My life is fettered with the chains of your love,
	Know it for certain, you are my devotion,
(*To Shasi*):	Take a drum and give the cymbals to Suryi. (*Bhadra plays on the violin and sings.*)
	Oh, my Lord! You are letting me
	Into the strong current of sorrow
	For no fault of mine.
	All is over for me in the world,
	My life is dipped in sorrow,

PADMAVATI: I feel like putting an end to my life,
Being scourged by pangs of sorrow;
Oh, my Lord! Lead me along
The right path I can't know.
Dear Bhadra and my dear sisters, my life is at your mercy. If your dear Padmavati had been living happily, I don't know how you could be soothing her life. Today, Padmavati is like a deer hunted by a hunter in a forest. She is as helpless as a deer fleeing for life when her horns are trapped among the creepers. How can she survive? I owe my life so long to you, my friends. I could have drowned myself in the waters of the Kaveri by now. (*crying*)

SHASI: (*rises quickly and wipes Padmavati's tears with the end of her sari.*) Please be quiet. How long will you cry? (*Wipes her tears. Bhadra and Suryi wipe their tears.*)

PADMAVATI: Shasi, it is not desirable that one would take birth in a royal family. Everybody wishes to be born into a royal family, but it's a greater sin. If you are born with good fortune, wherever you are, you are lucky. If it is not, it's unfortunate. Dear friend, let my lord not marry me but I would like to be his handmaid forever.

SHASI: Alas! How could he be so cruel to say that he would hand over such a gem to a sweeper?

PADMAVATI: Shasi, don't blame him. I know him well. Men like him, so judicious, generous and righteous, are rare. He might have said it out of disgust. He is not so cruel as to tell this about me. A man of flesh and blood can never be heartless, otherwise there would have been no trace of kindness in the world. The seed of love was implanted in me when I visited the king of Puri with my parents on the occasion of the Rath Yatra. When I saw him there, the seed of love in my heart germinated. I could realise that the lord my heart had become the lord of my life. While plucking flowers in the royal garden, I accidentally saw him. Out of shyness, I left the place. That occasion will never come in my life. (*shedding tears*) One day he visited us while taking *Mahaprasad*. As soon as I saw him, I fled and hid behind the doors and had *Mahaprasad* with our father. The memory of that incident often tortures me and I can no longer endure the intense pangs of separation. It's my ill luck. I am now a puppet in the hands of cosmic illusion. When I slip into the abysmal depth of misery, and be no more, pray in one voice with all your heart to the Almighty for divine bliss for my soul. If at all I rise to the top of

	the cycle of Destiny and enjoy good fortune, I shall confide in you a few things lurked in my heart. Convey my misery to the king of Odisha then. I am not as fortunate as a princess but only an unfortunate maiden. Oh my God! (*faints*)
BHADRA:	(*anxiously*) Bring some water.
SHASI AND SURYI:	What happened? (*Fetch water and sprinkle on Padma.*) How long will you suffer like this?
PADMAVATI:	Oh Bhadra! My lord is advancing for a war. So far, I was worried about myself but now I am worried about my parents. As the signs of Lord Ganesha indicate today, I have had a nightmare that my lord is defeated in the war and attempting to sacrifice his life. Alas! If my lord is defeated in the war, what will happen to me?
BHADRA:	Please, be quiet. Give up your worries. The Almighty will take of everything. You needn't worry.
PADMAVATI:	(*pathetically keeps quiet for a moment*) Bhadra, why do you worry? Why do you look sad?
BHADRA:	Padma, why do you worry? My heart aches thinking about your misery. The songs you were happily singing have evaporated into thin air because of your sorrow. My heart cries for you. Oh, virtuous one! You are still not completely revealing your heart.

PADMAVATI:	(*pathetically*) Yes. (*song*) How shall I reveal my heart, My heart is dipped in sorrow; If the tree flings the Malati away, Can Malati give up its warmth? My sorrows pile up, The Moon of my happiness is engulfed; Under them, my heart's buried I am like a lotus uprooted.
BHADRA:	What an enchanting voice! The Almighty is too cruel to put an end to it.
PADMAVATI:	Dear Bhadra, it's my misfortune. Let the Almighty's will prevail.
SHASI:	Let's not delay. Her Majesty will be angry with us.
PADMAVATI:	let's go. Dear Bhadra, consecrate my ears daily with your song.
BHADRA:	you needn't remind me. The world never forgets who belongs to whom. (*Curtain*)

SCENE V

(The Court Room in Kanchi. The king of Kanchi, Minister and courtiers are seated.)

KING:	(*Listening attentively for a while*) Can you hear any noise, minister? (*Low sound of war drums from the background*)
MINISTER:	(*Listening attentively for a while*) Yes, Your Majesty. It sounds like war drums from a long distance. (*sounds of war drums approaching*)
KING:	Isn't it the sound of war drums? Listen, to how quickly it comes closer.
MINISTER:	Yes, Your Majesty. Comes quickly closer ... towards us ... Is it the king of Odisha advancing?
CHIEF NOBLE:	So quickly? What is it? Slogan of Jaya Jagannath?
MINISTER:	Your Majesty, the king of Odisha has perhaps arrived.
KING:	What a wonder! Are our soldiers sleeping? (*tumultuous noise of war drums*)
MINISTER:	Your Majesty, please listen, our

KING:	soldiers are ready. Is it the repetition of Jaya Ganesh? Oh! Has the war started? (*anxiously hears*) (*Tumultuous noise of war songs and sounds of arms and ammunition from the background*)
MINISTER:	War has started.
KING:	Dear minister, let the court be adjourned. Let's go to the battlefield to encourage our soldiers, if necessary. If we are present there, misfortune if any, can be averted. (*A bustle of 'Jaya', 'Jaya' from the background*)
KING:	What is it? What is the implication of the sounds of "Jaya', 'Jaya' now? Has the battle come to an end so quickly? Let's all go. (*Stands up.*)
ALL:	(*Ready to leave.*) (*the guard arrives hurriedly.*)
GUARD:	Your Majesty, the Commander-in-chief is waiting at the door.
KING:	Commander-in-chief? Let him in.
GUARD:	Yes, Your Majesty.
MINISTER:	There might be good news, Your Majesty.
KING:	Let's see. (*All take their respective seats and the Commander-in-chief comes in.*)
COMMANDER-IN-CHIEF:	(*Bows down overwhelmingly.*) Glory be to the king of Kanchi! Jaya Lord Ganesha!

KING: (*The King Rises from his seat, joyfully embraces the Commander-in-chief and makes him sit to his left. Minister and all the nobles rise as the King rises, express their joy and take their seats after the King is seated.*)
Be quietly seated. Before listening to how the honour of the king of Kanchi has been safeguarded by this victory, I award this gold lotus pendant as a prize to the Commander-in-chief. (*Removes the pendent and places it around the neck of the Commander-in-chief.*) I too award him the title "Bajranada".

ALL: Glory be to the king of Kanchi. (*The Commander-in-chief joyfully bows his head.*)

KING: Now, Commander-in-chief, describe in detail what happened on the battlefield and please the court.

COMMANDER-IN-CHIEF: Your Majesty, the king of Kanchi, is greater than Lord Indra. As soon as Your Majesty's express commands were conveyed to us by the esteemed minister, we moved the army in battle order and set up our camp on the ground opposite Satakotipattana. We waited for two days but there was no commotion from the enemy. Half of our army was always keeping guard while the other half rested. We have not slept since we received the

	commands for war. We were waiting for the enemy within five to six miles of the city. Today at 10 a.m. as we advanced nearly one mile, we heard great commotion from a distance.
KING:	How far was the noise from you?
COMMANDER:	About two miles away.
KING:	Could you know that the king of Odisha was advancing?
COMMANDER:	Who will teach me about it, Your Majesty? This humble servant of the kingdom has attained the age of fifty in this service.
KING:	Thank you, Bajranada. Yes, what next?
COMMANDER:	As soon as we heard the commotion, I commanded the soldiers to be ready. Our soldiers are skilled, Your Majesty. Soon they were on their toes. The soldiers of Odisha were no less. They arrived very soon. Immediately, I commanded the battle drums to be beaten. Our soldiers jumped into the battle chanting 'Gana', 'Gana' loudly. The soldiers of Odisha were arranged in twenty files. What a wonderful sight! How skilfully they were trained! As soon as they heard the battle drums, they formed a triangle. Our soldiers were one and a half times larger in number than theirs. What can they do to us? Before they were ready,

	our soldiers penetrated one angle. Your Majesty might have heard the uproarious noise of 'Jaya', 'Jaya' that rose from us. The king of Odisha was humiliatingly swept away in the current of that noise.
KING:	(*Delightfully embraces the Commander once again.*) Thank you, Bajranada. You will be duly honoured for keeping up the honour of your king. I don't think that the king of Odisha has retreated. You should not be complacent. Be in readiness for a few days. Dear minister, announce our victory in the city. Command the subjects to desist from all work and to remain alert. When the hurly-burly is done, all merry-making, felicitation to the Commander-in-Chief and the worship of Lord Ganesha will be done.
MINISTER:	Yes, Your Majesty. (*about to leave*)
KING:	Yes, one more thing. Bring the prisoner here.
MINISTER:	Guard!
	(*"Yes, Your Majesty" is heard from the background. The guard enters.*)
MINISTER:	Bring the prisoner here.
GUARD:	Yes, Your Majesty. (*Exit.*)
KING:	No more work is pending now. Commander, you have duly kept up the honour of your king. Look, how audacious he is! He will degrade

me to less than a sweeper! He was boasting about handing over my dear daughter Padmavati to a sweeper! What is the status now? Less than a sweeper. (*The guard along with the prisoner with hands and feet in chains enters.*) Release him. (*The guard removes the chains. The messenger remains standing with folded hands.*)
Meghabarna! Your king is trounced and therefore, you too. Go to your people and shed tears. See for yourself who is less than a sweeper. Our desire has been fulfilled. There is no need to keep you as a prisoner any longer.

MEGHABARNA: As you please, Your Majesty. Let me take your leave. (*Bows and exit.*)

COMMANDER: You are very magnanimous, Your Majesty.

KING: Let the court be dismissed.
(*Curtain*)

ACT IV

SCENE I

(The kingdom of Kanchi. Mango grove. Purushottam Dev is seen kneeling with devotion under a tree with folded hands.)

KING: *(Pathetically)* Oh Lord, redeemer of the downtrodden! How dare I say that the banner of the redeemer of the downtrodden is being tarnished? My Lord, all my life this poor soul has offered prayers at your lotus feet and been blessed by a blissful life. I doubt whether the Lord, while in a meditative trance on the back of serpent Ananta, enjoys a better station than me. When I shed happy tears being overwhelmed by your blissful generosity, I feel my tears are holier than the holy water of rain. A beautiful blue hill is in front of me. The exquisite autumn moonbeam illuminates the whole earth and peeps through the sylvan foliage. The azure sky is studded with stars.

The luminous galaxy appears in the sky as a girdle. All these enchanting scenes of nature sing your glory, My Lord, don't they? I too sing your glory. But the difference is that they sing in joy but this poor soul in misery. (*sheds tears*) My Lord! while in death bed my father Kapilendra Deb was worried about his successor, you appeared in his dream and named me as your choice out of my eighteen brothers. After my father's demise, my step-brother used various means to kill me, you have saved this poor soul. When they bound my hand and feet and tried to throw me into the sea, you, My Lord, saved this wretch. All their attempts on my life failed because of your blessings on me. Out of frustration and despair, they all fled to distant lands in the west and south. My Lord, the king of Kanchi offended you. He called me a sweeper and ignored you. As I wished to avenge the wrong, you proceeded to the battlefield as a guide. If this is the consequence, if I have to be humiliated in the alien land, I have given up hope of my survival. My body will mingle with the soil of this place. I take refuge under your lotus feet. (*sheds tears and remains sitting in remorse with head downcast.*)

	(*A song in the background along with violin music.*)
	Can anyone in this whole world, Dear Padmavati,
	understand your sorrow? Is there any with pity?
	He that you doted on has cast you off,
	You lurk in shame on your lotus face,
	Wishing to breathe your last.
	A lotus blooms with a bright colour cheerfully on the clear water,
	Spreads its aroma everywhere
	Swinging in the tremulous air
	Who knows why the gentle wind
	Contended with its doting heart
	Blew hard with perfidious intent,
	Blighted its joy and broke its heart.
KING:	What a melodious song! What a mellifluous note! Which is the source of this sweet stream of music? From which moon-like lake does it flow? Who is so kind as to bring solace to this grieving heart? Let me find out the kind soul. Will this song be ever repeated? (*leaves the stage and comes back after a short while*) Is it a divine illusion? I could not see anybody. Why did cosmic illusion make me hear a song about Padmavati's misery? Who is Padmavati to me? Be calm, oh mind. Realise yourself and be quiet. I need not reveal my

heart so suddenly. It's not fair to tell now that you like Padmavati with all your heart. As a king you should never violate the oath you have taken. If you do that, your subordinates will condemn you. Taking the instance of your sin, they may indulge in nefarious activities. Padmavati, how much virtuous you might be, and how much inclined you might be to the king of Odisha, I am being condemned in this song. You are undone. You cannot fare well in this world. You will certainly be entrusted to a sweeper. Oh, Lord Jagannath! All my thoughts are in vain. Shall I be relegated to the hell of suffering in this state of humiliation and by forgiving one who defies the Lord? I won't get up from this place. There is no need for this life. (*falls down as if prostrating before the Lord*) (*Dasa enters*)

DASA: Glory be to the King. Why does Your Majesty look miserable?

KING: (*Pathetically*) Dasa, I don't feel like living any longer. Even though both Lord Jagannath and Lord Balabhadra were present, even though the Almighty Lord of the Universe helped me, I suffered defeat, indignity and humiliation. I now understand that My Lord has

	forsaken me. I no longer enjoy the Lord's affection, mercy and love. I am a great sinner. So I shall sacrifice my sinful life here. (*sheds tears*)
DASA:	You are right in your repentance. You have had your due atonement. Your Majesty need not worry; you have the Lord's mandate.
KING:	What is the Lord's mandate, Dasa? What is the Lord's mandate to this sinner?
DASA:	It's the Lord's mandate that you should resume the battle tomorrow morning.
KING:	(*Suddenly rising*) Shall we resume the battle tomorrow morning? Is the Lord again putting me under the test? Lord's commands must be carried out. Alas! What was my fault that I had to suffer so much humiliation?
DASA:	I had the vision in my dream that when Your Majesty had learnt from Maniki that the Lords are taking part in the war on your behalf, you boasted that you are more privileged than Lord Brahma. Therefore, the Lord was angry with you. The Lord is now satisfied with Your Majesty's repentance and has commanded you to resume the battle and please yourself.
KING:	(*Heaving a deep sigh*) Glory be to Lord Jagannath. This wretched heart is

	relieved. What is done is done. I cannot forget what has happened due to a small fault of mine. If you had not come with me, I could not have got this mandate. You were not willing to come.
DASA:	It's your kindness, Your Majesty. (*Jester enters.*)
JESTER:	(*gleefully*) Your Majesty, the fruit has ripened on the tree.
KING:	What pleasure! Which fruit?
JESTER:	Edible fruit.
KING:	Then, it's a nice fruit. For whom? Whose tree?
JESTER:	War is the fruit. The consumer is *Gopala Chudamani* himself.
KING:	How do you become *Gopala Chudamani*?
JESTER:	I should have added a footnote to it, Your Majesty. I forgot out of joy. Your Majesty, *Gopala* means curd, *Chuda* means flattened rice and *mani* means molasses. One whose body is made up of these three things loves them. (*laughs*)
DASA:	(*laughing loudly*) How funny you are!
KING:	(*laughing*) What ready wit! How could you know that it was ripe?
JESTER:	Should I elaborate on it? When Dasa just dropped a hint, Commander Birabal and the soldiers went out of control. They are boating in the waters of joy. (*Birabal enters.*) Yes, Birabal has come at the right time.

KING: What is the news, Birabal?
BIRABAL: God news, Your Majesty. Let Your Majesty please see how the minds of our soldiers are fortified. (*The royal preceptor enters.*)
PRECEPTOR: (*recites auspicious chants.*) The demon is sure to go to hell. There is no reason to worry. It's all propitious for Your Majesty.
KING: Let's then go and inspire the soldiers. (*Curtain*)

SCENE II

(The inner apartment in the royal palace of Kanchi. King Kalabareswar and Queen Bidyullata are seated on the bed.)

KING: What will happen now? All of a sudden two swords flashed and and cut down our soldiers. What will happen now? What will happen to Padma? Oh, Lord Ganesha! Is it the end of our destiny? How could I carry out your mandate in my dream? Had I opted for a truce, I would have surrendered Padmavati. Well, since I have not obeyed the mandate, I have to accept what may come. The fate of the unfortunate is never straight. I am very much worried about Padma. Can we be safe from the clutches of the enemy if we flee into the forest with Padma? Oh, Lord Ganesha! Oh, my bad fate! Padma has to suffer so much for us. What can be done now? The scoundrel will now send his men to us. Alas! What a sad fate! What an unfortunate girl! *(cries bitterly)*

QUEEN:	(*sheds tears and wipes them with the end of her sari*) My dear Padma! (*cries bitterly*)
	(*Padmavati enters crying*)
KING:	(*cries loudly*) My dear Padma! My dear daughter! (*faints*)
QUEEN:	(*rises crying*) Now, dear Padma …. (*faints*)
PADMAVATI:	Father! Mother! (*faints*)
VOICE:	(*from within*) Suryi! Run! Fetch some water.
	(*Shasikala, Suryabala and Bhadra enter with a pot of water and try to bring them back to sense.*)
PADMAVATI:	Dear Shasi, Suryi and Bhadra! This is the end of my life. Dear friends, don't forget me.
	(*leans on Shasikala and cries*)
SHASI, SURYI AND BHADRA:	(*cry surrounding Padma and trying to console her*) Please be quiet.
	(*King is miserable and sits with his head downcast.*)
QUEEN:	Dear Padma! Come to me. (*stretches her hands*)
PADMAVATI:	(*aside*) What can be done? If I meet the lord of my life, I shall humbly appeal to him that without me my ageing parents will be miserable.
QUEEN:	Come to me, my dear! I feel restless without you.
	(*Padmavati approaches her mother, and suddenly four soldiers hurriedly enter.*)

1ST SOLDIER:	Here is Padmavati. Capture her.
2ND SOLDIER:	Yes, let's take her with us without delay. (*Try to catch hold of Padmavati.*)
KING:	(*looking at the soldiers with anger*) Where is my sword? (*trying to get up faints.*)
QUEEN:	What happened to you? (*trying to get up faints.*)
SHASI, SURYI AND BHADRA:	What has happened to us? (*cry bitterly*)
ALL SOLDIERS:	Jaya Jagannath! Now, Padmavati is arrested. (*try to capture Padmavati.*)
PADMAVATI:	(*crying bitterly*) Oh, my God! Ah, father! Ah, mother! I am the only helpless daughter of my parents. How can you … … (*faints*) (*Soldiers are perplexed and stand away from her*)
SHASI, SURYI AND BHADRA:	What happened? What happened? (*try to bring Padma to her senses*) Padmavati: (*coming back to senses*) Shasi, Suryi, my dear parents! (*cries*)
1ST SOLDIER:	Hold her. Let's go.
ALL SOLDIERS:	Let's go. (*one of the soldiers tries to get Padmavati up, all of them surround her and exit*)
PADMAVATI:	Soldier, excuse me. Let go of my hand. (*furiously*) You brute! How dare you touch my sacred body? You will reap its consequences. Leave my hand. (*draws her hand back*) Let

me have a last glance at my parents. Dear Shasi, Suryi and Bhadra, why do you follow me? I am a luckless, miserable prisoner. Why do you cry piteously and follow me? If God will, all will be well. Look at my parent; how miserable they are! Bring them back to their senses and console them. Who is there to look after them? If all of you accompany me, how can they survive? (*cries, and holding Shasikala's chin*) Shasi, please tell them not to worry about me. God is above us! Bye, friends. I greet you all. (*embraces each of them sorrowfully*)

SHASIKALA: (*embracing and crying*) Are you leaving, dear?

BHADRA: (*holding Padma's chin*) Are leaving the palace in darkness?
(*Song*)
As *bheri* is sounded in Braja's arena,
Orphaned have turned Gopa's women.

PADMAVATI: (*Putting her hand on Padmavati's shoulders*) My dear Padma, how can we live without you? Oh My God!
I am leaving, Bhadra. Shasi, please look after my parents. Convey my regards to them. (*As she bows her head a few drops of tears roll down and Padma wipes them.*) I could not see them properly. Shasi, keep this dear

friend of yours in mind. Preserve all my toys and other things dear to me. Dear Suryi! Dear Bhadra! Forgive me. We will certainly meet again if I survive. Bye! *(leaves the place crying surrounded by soldiers.)*

BHADRA: Shasi, what do you look at? Stand between them. Suryi, leave immediately and bring a pot of cool water. *(Suryabala exits. Shasi stands beside the king and the queen shedding tears.)*

BHADRA: Shasi, I can't take heart.
(Song)
Shall the souls be ever together?
How can I alone live here, my dear?
Pour oil on the sacrificial fire,
Shall it ever burn dimmer, my dear?
Better to die than by poison,
Can one be glad by gliding on waves, my dear?
Can a fresh green leaf from the tree sever
Be happy and not wither, my dear?
The princess in the morn, a prisoner on the eve,
Will the happy days come ever, my dear?
(Suryabala enters with a pot of water.)
Attend on the King and the Queen; hurry up.
(Curtain)

ACT V

SCENE I

(Puri. The Drawing Room of the Royal Palace. King Purushottam Dev, Minister Bidyanidhi, Jester, Commander Birabal, the Preceptor, Dasa and the courtiers are seated.)

JESTER:	Your Majesty, how beautiful this place looks! I doubt if Puri has ever witnessed such a marvellous courtroom scene. The excellent beds, the beautiful chandeliers and very rare collections. The banquet hosted by Your Majesty has added to the magnificence. Once the stomach is satisfied, there is eternal peace.
BIRABAL:	So, you have had a full meal.
MINISTER:	[*making a pun on the full meal (Purna Grasa in Odia means 'a full meal' and 'total solar eclipse in English*)] It is a total solar eclipse; the earth is submerged in darkness.
JESTER:	Esteemed minister, because of the full meal, this drawing room, this luxury, this wonderful light arrange-

	ment appear wonderful. Your wit is working in your brain, so everything appears dark to you. If you were walking with your leg, you would see everything clearly. (*laughs*)
PRECEPTOR:	(*in a lighter vein*) You take it amiss, Natabar. During the total eclipse, the earth is under darkness. Only when the eclipse is over and the sun appears, does everything look bright.
MINISTER:	(*in a lighter vein*) Now Natabar has to admit defeat.
JESTER:	Yes, why not? Our Gurudev is very wise. (*laughs*) There is no limit to his miraculous powers. If he likes, he can produce a flood in a river during winter.
KING:	Yes, indeed! The miraculous powers of Gurudev were not known earlier. I am pleased with him for the way he has saved our honour in times of adversity. I declare in this court that I award him the tenancy of village Balapur to enjoy tax-free for generations. He will henceforth be known as Godabari Mishra.
PRECEPTOR:	It adds to the glory of Your Majesty.
MINISTER:	Your Majesty! Most of us are not aware of that wonderful incident. If commanded, someone can elaborate on it.
KING:	It is destiny. Godabari is very far from Kanchipur. When we have

demolished the entire army of Kanchi, it is beyond imagination how the King could organise so quickly more than one lakh soldiers to pursue us. Glory be to his filial affection! We have, of course, sent Birabal along with Padmavati and soldiers ahead of us. It's all due to the blessings of Lord Jagannath.

JESTER: Your Majesty! When Gurudev was in a hurry to deliver the message that the soldiers of Kanchi are chasing us, I could not understand the predicament. By that time the soldiers of Kanchi have assembled on the other bank of River Godavari. The King was worried and appealed to Gurudev, "I am undone! Devise some means to save us." Esteemed Mishra said, "All right" and went away. I thought that the old Brahmin was trying to play some pranks. I followed him and saw that Gurudev was sitting cross-legged under a tree with eyes closed and was chanting incantations. While the army of Kanchi was making a hue and cry with battle songs I thought if Gurudev was trying to bring the sky down with a stick. Your Majesty! What should I say? When the advancing soldiers were midway into the river, there came a flash flood and swept the entire army away into the Kingdom of Death. The king of Kanchi fled. Had he lingered a little while he too would have been swept into the sea. Esteemed Mishra had told me to wake him up when he was neck-deep in water. While water was rising to his neck, there was no trace of the king of Kanchi and his army. I called out to esteemed Mishra and he got up. The river was as calm as it was before. Your Majesty! Such a miracle had never occurred before.

MINISTER: How wonderful!

KING: Well, Dasa! Is the door sealed?

DASA: It has been sealed in the presence of the minister.

MINISTER: Yes, Your Majesty.

DASA: Your Majesty, it's not clear why the precious stones, gems and pearls collected from Kanchi as spoils from the war have been preserved in a closed room.

KING: Try to understand, Dasa, we are not in want at present. The wealth is secured because if at any time due to natural calamity, we encounter misfortune and there is no way out, people will break open the house. We have expressed our desire before the Lord and therefore, we are having a seven-day celebration.

JESTER: But, Your Majesty, this greedy Brah-

	min had thought that we would get a few stones for ourselves. (*Laughs.*)
DASA:	Well, what else do you need?
JESTER:	His Majesty had a great celebration. Had he not arranged a great feast, you would not have attended it.
KING:	What? Wouldn't you have attended the celebration for such a triviality?
JESTER:	Your Majesty, it is not a small matter. It is the most significant thing. A meal is bad without ghee. I had kept my stomach clean for the feast. (*Laughs.*)
MINISTER:	Is the earth in peace now?
JESTER:	You, too. (*Laughs.*)
KING:	Well, Dasa, one more thing, did you install the image of Bhanda Ganesha and Sakshi Gopal properly?
DASA:	Yes, Your Majesty. Bhanda Ganesha is installed in front of the temple of Goddess Bimala and at the back of God Narasingha. The place accommodated it well. All can behold the god properly. The image of Lord Gopal has been installed at Satyabadi. Our sculptors are so competent, Your Majesty, that they have built a marvellous temple within a few days. Lord Gopal adorned the south gate of the royal palace of Kanchi. Now as a witness of the war, He is beautifully seated at Satyabadi.
KING:	Very good. Such smartness is appre-

	ciable. Dear Minister, what are the programmes of entertainment for the subjects?
MINISTER:	Your Majesty, there are dance festivals in various parts of the city.
JESTER:	Then, Neelachal Puri must not be on earth.
MINISTER:	It's exactly so. Due to the blessings of Lord Jagannath it has got the status of Paradise. All the people of the court are making merry. We are waiting for Your Majesty's for today's program of entertainment which will be far better than those of the previous six days.
KING:	what is the program? Have the dancers come? Bring them in.
JESTER:	Yes, the sooner, the better.
MINISTER:	Guard!
Voice from the background:	"Your Majesty!" (*the guard enters.*)
MINISTER:	Call the dancers.
GUARD:	Yes, Your Majesty! (*Exit.*)
	(*Jester adjusts himself.*)
KING:	Mr. Acharya, Why are you getting ready?
PRECEPTOR:	He might dance.
JESTER:	Well, you have a bellyful of wisdom, as it were a shipload of learning. (*laughs.*) Your Majesty! I am sitting like a gentleman to enjoy the dance. I was groping for the rewards for the dancers. (*laughs.*)

	(Two dancers with their troupe enter, bow and wait.) The moon rises.
PRECEPTOR:	Then the earth bathes in moonbeam!
JESTER:	What shall I say more? Will they take some time?
KING:	No. Let the dance begin.
JESTER:	Begin your dance. Try to please me.

(Dancers begin their dance along with a song.)

(Song)
Sreekhetra is making merry,
the din of joy is so intense
As a festive paradise.
Rich and poor, all alike,
Are oblivious to agony and woes
And free from mundane cares.
The bustle of joy
Like sea waves huge
Heavenward rise,
Agitate the gods in paradise,
With a desire to be born on earth.
Denizens of Neelachal in pious delight
Chant God's name loud and thrilled
Shaking paradise in pure delight.
Glory be to Neelachal,
The Pride of Three Worlds,
The seat of Lord Jagannath,
The Lord of the Universe.

JESTER:	Very beautiful! *(flings five coins towards the dancers.)*

(Curtain)

SCENE II

(The royal bed chamber. King Purushottam Dev is lying on his bed.)

KING: *(Suddenly gets up and wipes his eyes.)* Oh! My God! What a nightmare! Oh God, why do you put this poor man into this deadly crisis and make him suffer? Can't I forget by any means what I try to wipe out from my mind? What a misery! Where is peace? Is Padmavati entrusted to a sweeper? She will cry bitterly. She will suffer hell for the deed of her father. Why does she appear in my dream now? Why do I dream of her that she is silently shedding tears while making a garland for me and putting it around my neck with much adoration? While kissing her, she suddenly disappeared. See, I have a sword in my hand! *(pause)* Again Padmavati! Again, as a sweeper woman! What a misfortune! Such a horrible dream is not the outcome of a simple thought about her. Oh, that war with

Kanchikaveri! Oh, the glory of Lord Jagannath! Oh, that Padmavati, and all those! War at one place, love at another!oh Oh God! If You derive pleasure by scorching my heart with needless misfortune, I have to humbly court it. Ah, Padmavati! Never blame the king of Odisha. He loves you with all his heart. Only if I could open my heart to you, as Lord Hanuman did to show that his heart is filled with the names of Lord Rama! Oh, how can I help it? Padmavati, it's all your father's fault. Had he not undermined Lord Jagannath, we would have a blissful world. Oh, shameless mind, why do you recollect it? isn't there a woman on earth more beautiful than Padmavati? Is Padmavati unique? Is she matchless? Isn't the minister's house visited by many people? Aren't there many beautiful women at his place? Why was I thunderstruck at the sight of Padmavati when she appeared on the terrace of the minister's palace? Fie on me! Such a weakness of mine is unpardonable. He has the King's orders. Would he so long keep her in his house without giving her away to a sweeper? Would he not be executed if he defied the King's orders? It's a wonder that all the subjects support Padmavati and condemn me. Wouldn't these people condemn me if I did not give her away to a sweeper and married myself? Thank them! Who would like to be your king? Traitors! (*tries to listen for a while*) What is it? What a mellifluous voice! What a melodious note!

(*A song on the violin from the background.*)

All male hearts are as hard as stone
You are destined, my friend, for your love to pine.
The one you courted as your better half
Gives you away to a sweeper,
As a necklace around the neck of a frog
You appear beside a sweeper.
Glory be to Lily, and glory be to Lotus as well,
They enjoy love divine, who can thus avail?
The wisest man on earth put your love to an end,
Pangs of separation stung you as the fangs of a serpent
To suffer the worst alone, Padmavati's left.

KING: What melodious numbers? Oh, the ripples of melody cool my ears and dance in the arena of my mind. Let my troubled mind be pacified a little. Ah! I feel I have heard this voice

	before. (*Thinks for a while*) I have heard it at Kanchi before the second battle. Alas! What a daring act has been done! All the denizens of the city have been shedding tears for Padmavati. All the people of the kingdom are condemning me for the sake of Padmavati. I too have been her affliction while being deeply in love with her. Alas! I am still full of remorse for her. Let bygones be bygones! Guard!
BACKGROUND VOICE:	Your Majesty! (*Guard enters.*)
KING:	See, who is singing at this hour of the night? Bring her here.
GUARD:	Yes, Your Majesty! (*Guard enters and renters after a while with Bhadra.*) (*Bhadra stands before the King with all humility.*)
KING:	Was this lady singing the song? Yes, it seemed like a female voice.
GUARD:	Yes, Your Majesty!
KING:	Well, you may go. (*the guard exits.*) (*To Bhadra*) Please be seated. Were you singing at this hour of the night?
BHADRA:	(*Taking her seat.*) Yes, Your Majesty!
KING:	What is your name?
BHADRA:	Bhadra.
KING:	Where do you come from?
BHADRA:	Kanchipuram.
KING:	(*Taken aback*) Kanchipuram! What brings you here?

The Conquest of Kanchi | 115

BHADRA: (*with folded hands*) Your Majesty! You don't know me. I am Padmavati's chorister. I'm a Vaishnavi and her bosom friend. I have been nourished by her, with her generosity. As she has been brought here as a prisoner, her two maidens and I have followed her. We learn that it's Your Majesty's orders that she has to marry a sweeper. But we are unable to know which sweeper she has been handed over to. The minister also doesn't reveal that. Your Majesty! I don't know where my two friends have gone. I am alone to sing her glory and misery at this Shree Kshetra. If I don't find her, I shall jump into the sea. (*wipes her tears with the end of her sari.*)

KING: Ah! You are indeed Padmavati's true companion.

BHADRA: Your Majesty! What shall I tell you? You might not believe what I would say. You are not aware that she adores you very much. Despite the fierce battle, humiliation and fear of being surrendered to a sweeper, being snatched away from the parents, the miserable wretch has never spoken ill of you. But your Majesty … … (*sheds tears*)

KING: Oh, Bhadra, is it for that reason you were condemning me? Before this,

	you were moving around our camp on the night after the first battle, and singing your song and condemning me, weren't you?
BHADRA:	(*aside*) I need not admit it now. God knows whether my efforts will bear fruits.
KING:	But, oh Bhadra, I don't think you should blame me for this. I know Padmavati very well. It's well known that Padmavati is not only simple but also wise. But who can prevent destiny?
BHADRA:	We too suffer because of her.
KING:	Because of her? Oh Bhadra, but for my promise, I was determined to marry Padmavati. I shall never marry in this life. By deserting Padmavati I have been thrown into a whirlpool of misery. My whole body is on fire as I hear Padmavati's pious love for me. She only is my wife for this birth. I have nothing more to say, Oh Bhadra, you may come now. But please, don't ever sing a song denigrating me and torture me. (*heaves a deep sigh*)
BHADRA:	(*aside*) All is well. Oh Padma, don't be miserable. Your darling is yours. The Krishna you had lost is ready to prostrate before you. My desire is fulfilled. Oh, fear fades from me. How do I bother about you now?

	Don't worry, wait for Krishna to come to you.
KING:	What do you brood over?
BHADRA:	I thought that it is only for their anger people suffer a lot and be repentant. it is heartening that Your Majesty has not yet given away Padmavati to a sweeper. I feel like laughing as well as crying at the same time when I hear that Your Majesty was in love with Padmavati.
KING:	Why crying then?
BHADRA:	It's because had she been the queen, we would have enjoyed good fortune. Your Majesty, there should have been a lot of merriment in the palace. The king of Kanchi would have surrendered himself to Lord Jagannath. He, of course, is His loving child. We have now lost everything. (*sheds tears and wipes them with the end of her sari.*)
KING:	(*Being quiet for some time heaves a deep sigh.*) Oh Bhadra, don't add salt to my injury. I am very much worried. You may go now. Let me rest a while. (*Sees off Padma and goes to bed.*) (*Bhadra exits*) (*Curtain*)

SCENE III

(The front arena of the temple of Lord Jagannath. Sounds of conch shells, bells, and trumpets. Servitors are shouting 'Haribol' and taking the Lord to his chariot following the 'Pahandi' ritual. Purushottam Dev is sweeping the ground before the Lord with a broom of gold sticks. The subjects are shouting 'Haribol' gleefully on either side of the King. The cacophony of women ululating is heard from the background. All of a sudden, Minister Bidyanidhi along with Padmavati and her maids enters. All noise subsides. All are stupefied.)

KING: *(with surprise and irritation)* Oh Minister! What is it? Why have you come here along with Padmavati? Oh fiend! You dared to defy my orders discreetly and now shamelessly appear at this consecrated place with Padmavati to present her to Lord Jagannath. It's a holy place, so I pardon you. Your case will be decided later. *(Padmavati casts a loving glance at the angry face of the King and is downcast with remorse and fright.)*

MINISTER: *(with folded hands)* Your Majesty! I beg your pardon. Please be calm. This poor man is going to submit his account. Everyone present here is aware of how this loyal subject has enjoyed your Majesty's favour by carrying out the royal commands. It is not only impertinent but also impossible that I have tacitly defied the royal orders without any relevant reasons and have now appeared brazen-faced before Your Majesty. Your Majesty knows this Bidyanidhi well; how loyal and humble he is. Moreover, your Majesty is the only witness to how peace has prevailed in the kingdom in your absence. The world is not eternal. Therefore, everything in this world is ephemeral. When human beings as sizzling with the poison of evil instincts like greed, violence and malice, why should one willfully indulge in an unlawful act? Whoever does that is the worst scoundrel. Your Majesty! I have not defied the royal mandate. If a tender creeper grows luxuriantly in a jungle, can it dedicate its life to a mean shrub? Will Goddess Lakshmi, who rose from the churning of the seas, head for the earth? The subjects of the capital city and even the whole state being upset by the cruel royal orders are commiserating with Princess Padmavati, and offering their prayers to the Lord. Princess

Padmavati, a paragon with beauty and noble virtues, is destined for a royal house. Can nectar-like delicious milk which is fit for the wealthy to relish be given away to a scavenger? Your Majesty, the severe royal orders were given in a fury. Even though the severe oath was taken in an angry mood, you have tenaciously honoured it as a kingly duty. Your Majesty, it's the bounden duty of this humble servant to carry out the royal orders issued to him. The orders I received made the courtiers so remorseful that the court was dismissed in a hurry. Your Majesty, this humble creature has since then been deliberating on the means of carrying out such an anti-people order. I have got the right opportunity now. I have been heartbroken to hear how the princess has been through tremendous suffering owing to separation from you since the day she courted Your Majesty as her lord when she first came here. I could not but be compassionate to her. This humble creature cannot comprehend if Your Majesty would be able to hold patience to listen to her long tale of woe. Your Majesty, under these circumstances, this humble creature could not carry out the royal orders.

Now, you have the broomstick in your hand. In the meantime, the king of Kanchi has come here and atoned for his sins. He has prostrated before Lord Jagannath and accepted Him as the Lord of the Universe. It seems that Lord Jagannath has been pleased with his atonement. Accepting his prayers Lord Jagannath has been in the regalia of elephant face on the *Snana Purnima* Day. The king of Kanchi only said He is omnipresent. We should not denigrate Him. All the gods and goddesses worship Him and He is in all forms. Therefore, the reason for disharmony has been resolved. We should be generous to an enemy who admits defeat. Moreover, the Queen of Kanchi overwhelmed with sorrow for the misery of the princess has been shedding tears day in and day out, and waiting for Your Majesty's magnanimity. However, Your Majesty has the broom of gold sticks in your hand. This innocent Princess, Padmavati, (*bringing Padmavati to his front*) is present here in the presence of Lord Jagannath and this huge mankind for punishment or reward due to her. It's for you, Your Majesty, to protect or punish her. I offer myself for my due punishment if I so deserve it. However, in obedience to royal orders, this humble creature on behalf of the people present here and in the presence of Lord Jagannath offers Princess Padmavati to the right sweeper. I lay my humble prayers before Your Majesty. (*bursts into tears*)

ALL: (*in unison*): Hail the minister! Long live King Purushottam Dev, the magnanimous ruler of subjects. (*A joyous hue and cry.*)

(*The King casts a glance at the minister, holds Padmavati's right hand in his left and draws her towards him. There is a deafening noise of Jaya Jagannath, 'Haribol', ululation of women, and musical instruments. The Pahandi activities resume.*)

(*A Song from the background*)
Today is the day for all to rejoice,
The queen of Odisha is the Kanchi princess,
King Purushottam is her deserving spouse,
All conflicts did hopefully resolve
Lord Jagannath is the Lord of the Universe.
Happy is Padmavati, and happy her parents,
Happy bosom Bhadra, and happy all subjects.

Hail Minister Bidyanidhi, for his loving care,
The audience is happy with merry cheer,
Shout 'Haribol' for general welfare,
Long live Purushottam, Odisha's ruler.

Jay Jagannath, the Lord of the Universe,
Glory be to the Lord, the Lord of the Universe.
(Curtain)

Black Eagle Books

www.blackeaglebooks.org
info@blackeaglebooks.org

Black Eagle Books, an independent publisher, was founded as a nonprofit organization in April, 2019. It is our mission to connect and engage the Indian diaspora and the world at large with the best of works of world literature published on a collaborative platform, with special emphasis on foregrounding Contemporary Classics and New Writing.

www.ingramcontent.com/pod-product-compliance
Lightning Source LLC
Chambersburg PA
CBHW060615080526
44585CB00013B/842